PADDINGTON TO PRINCES RISBOROUGH

Vic Mitchell and Keith Smith

MP Middleton Press

Cover picture: No. 6029 King Edward VIII *starts the six-mile climb over the Chilterns as it leaves High Wycombe on 13th January 1962. The chocolate and cream coaches form the down "Cambrian Coast Express" to Aberystwyth and Pwllheli. (B.Jennings)*

Published April 2002
First reprint June 2006

ISBN 1 901706 81 8

© Middleton Press 2002

Design   Deborah Esher
Typesetting Barbara Mitchell

Published by
          Middleton Press
          Easebourne Lane
          Midhurst, West Sussex
          GU29 9AZ
Tel: 01730 813169
Fax: 01730 812601
Email: info@middletonpress.co.uk
www.middletonpress.com

Printed and bound by Biddles Ltd, King's Lynn

CONTENTS

ACKNOWLEDGEMENTS

Our sincere gratitude goes to so many of the photographers who have helped us and also to A.E.Bennett, W.R.Burton, R.M.Casserley, G.Croughton, M.Dart, J.C.Gillham, N.Langridge, J.H.Meredith, Mr D. and Dr S.Salter, G.T.V.Stacey, D.Wilson, E.Youldon and especially our wives.

I. GWR map of 1910 (GWR Magazine)

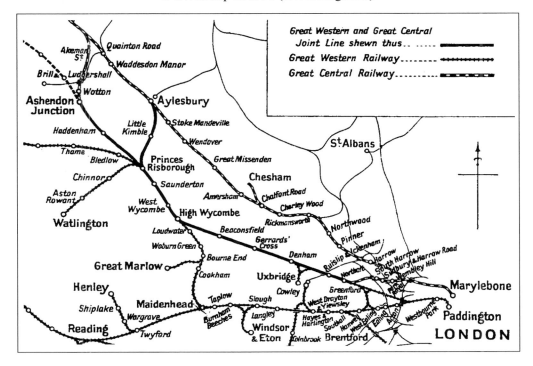

GEOGRAPHICAL SETTING

The route is almost entirely on London Clay from Paddington to Denham. It crosses the shallow valleys of the River Brent (near Perivale), the River Colne (east of Denham) and the Misbourne River east of Gerrards Cross. The Uxbridge branch is entirely in the Colne Valley.

In the vicinity of Gerrards Cross and Beaconsfield, the line traverses the Reading Beds, which comprise sand, clay and pebbles.

On entering the Wye Valley, east of High Wycombe, the tracks were laid over the Chalk of the Chiltern Hills.

The route remains on Chalk until leaving the Chilterns on its descent into Princes Risborough, down the scarp slope of the Hills.

The maps are to the scale of 25ins to 1 mile, unless otherwise stated.

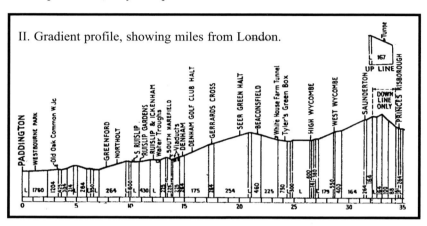

II. Gradient profile, showing miles from London.

HISTORICAL BACKGROUND

The Wycombe Railway opened a single line broad gauge branch from the 1838 Maidenhead station to High Wycombe on 1st August 1854. It was extended to Thame on 1st August 1862 and a branch from Princes Risborough to Aylesbury was added in 1863. These lines were converted to standard gauge in 1870, having become part of the Great Western Railway in 1867. They were all operated by the GWR from the outset. A branch from Princes Risborough to Watlington came into use in 1872.

The Great Central Railway had gained access to its new terminus at Marylebone by making arrangements in 1899 to run over the Metropolitan Railway via Aylesbury and Amersham. This was deemed to be unsatisfactory and so the GCR made plans with the GWR for a new joint line of double track south-east from High Wycombe to Northolt Junction. Here the GCR built eastwards, while the GWR laid double track to a junction with its 1838 main line from

Paddington, near Old Oak Common. These lines came into full use on 2nd April 1906, although Park Royal was open for passengers from 3rd June 1903 for five weeks to serve an agricultural show and goods traffic on the route began in November 1905.

The GWR also built the Greenford Loop between Greenford and West Ealing, with triangular junctions at each end. Services began between those two places on 1st October 1904.

The new main line was completed by doubling the track between High Wycombe and Princes Risborough. The GWR's distance between London and Birmingham was thus reduced, as trains could run via Thame and Oxford. It was shortened further in 1910, when a new line from Princes Risborough via Bicester was completed to Aynho Junction.

A branch south from the joint line to Uxbridge (High Street) was opened by the GWR for passengers on 1st May 1907 and for goods on 11th May 1914. It was closed completely on 1st January 1917 and reopened as single track on 3rd May 1920. Another wartime closure followed: passenger services ceased on 1st September 1939, permanently. However, freight continued until 24th February 1964.

The GWR promoted the Ealing & Shepherds Bush Railway in 1905 to branch north from its main line at Ealing to provide a freight link with the West London Line, north of Kensington. Delayed by the war, it opened for its intended purpose on 16th April 1917. It was electrified and used by Central London Railway underground trains between Wood Lane and Ealing Broadway from 3rd August 1920. The section between North Acton and the WLL was quadrupled on 19th June 1938, as it could not accommodate both types of traffic, as tube train frequency was planned to increase.

Upon nationalisation in 1948, the route became part of the Western Region of British Railways, although the Marylebone services were operated by the Eastern Region, having been worked by London & North Eastern Railway trains since 1923. These were transferred to the London Midland Region on 1st February 1958 and to the Western Region on 24th March 1973.

The route became part of Network SouthEast in 1986 and was privatised on 21st July 1996 to be operated by Chiltern Railways. A seven-year franchise was let to M40 Trains Ltd and on 19th February 2002, it became the first to be extended by 20 years.

Details of the opening of the lines associated with the three miles at the London end of the route are given in the relevant map captions. Freight service withdrawals are noted in captions for the associated pictures.

This increase was due to London Transport (established in 1933) proposing to extend its Central Line operation to West Ruislip from a junction at North Acton. The planned route ran parallel to the 1906 main line and its construction was undertaken by the GWR. Delayed by World War II, the North Acton to Greenford section came into use on 30th June 1947 and the extension to West Ruislip followed on 21st November 1948. Most intermediate GWR stations and halts were then closed.

III. The Wycombe Railway and later developments. (Railway Magazine)

PASSENGER SERVICES

Down trains running on at least five weekdays are listed below. Those prior to 1906 started at Maidenhead or Paddington and ran to Aylesbury or Oxford in most cases. Those after 1906 originated mainly at Marylebone or at Paddington, although a few continued to run from or via Maidenhead until 1969. Some proceeded to Oxford or the Midlands.

| | High Wycombe | | Princes Risborough | |
	Weekdays	**Sundays**	**Weekdays**	**Sundays**
1869	4	3	4	3
1885	8	3	7	2
1901	13	4	7	2
1913	30	15	18	5
1933	30	25	9	8

Major changes began in 1961 when diesel services started and in June 1962 the shuttle autotrain on the Aylesbury branch was replaced by a regular interval service from Marylebone. Thereafter Paddington departures were limited to about six expresses for the Midlands or beyond, generally only stopping at High Wycombe. By 1974, there was only one (at 17.40).

There was still only one in 2002 (at 10.51), it being used for crew route familiarisation for emergencies, and for legal reasons to keep the route technically open.

GWR suburban services

One railmotor was provided to run a 70-minute interval service of 14 trips per weekday between Park Royal and Hanwell, via the Greenford Loop, from 1st July 1904. From 1st October of that year, a second one was introduced and both served Greenford where they had to reverse. They started at Westbourne Park and ran via Park Royal; one continued to Hanwell and the other to Acton, this running on to Willesden Junction on seven of its ten trips. Hanwell proved unremunerative and ceased to be served regularly on 10th October 1905. The Willesden Junction trains were discontinued in the previous month and the experiments ended on 1st July 1906, after which date Park Royal received 13 trains each weekday. Most started at Westbourne Park (Paddington was too congested) and ran via Greenford to Ealing or Acton.

A third railmotor was needed when the Uxbridge branch opened on 1st July 1907. It reversed at Denham and started two trips at Greenford, two at Willesden Junction, one at West Ealing and one at Acton. From October of that year, one started from Southall (the depot was there). This complicated scheme was soon abandoned and the branch railmotor shuttled to and from Denham; soon most journeys were extended to Gerrards Cross. The service was intended to give Uxbridge connections with trains northwards and not to London.

Railmotors or autotrains supplemented conventional trains as far out as Beaconsfield until 1947, the pattern of operation being most complex. In the early years, most ran from Paddington (or Westbourne Park) via Ealing and the Greenford Loop, while longer distance trains took the direct route. There were also railmotors on this line serving the halts and terminating at West Ealing or Greenford (or stations west thereof, Northolt in particular from 1932).

Local services were withdrawn with the advent of electrification of the route to West Ruislip for LT trains in 1947-48.

Sample train frequencies to Uxbridge High Street are thus:

	Weekdays	**Sundays**
August 1908	9	11
March 1909	9	6
July 1910	9	10
June 1922	12	-
August 1939	9	-

For most of the 1930s, trains ran in the peak hours only.

June 1922

LONDON, HIGH WYCOMBE, and PRINCES RISBORO'.—G. W. & G. C.

Down. — Week Days.

Miles	Station	mrn	mrn	mrn	mrn	mrn	mrn	mrn	mrn	mrn	aft	aft	aft	aft	aft	aft	aft	aft	aft
	Paddington ....dep.					8	129	10	9	5		1223		1 26			2 2		5 53
1¼	Westbourne Park						132		9											
4¾	Acton *					8	21		9	16										4 4
5¼	Ealing (Broadway) †					8	23		9	25										4 7
6¼	West Ealing					8	25		9	25			1244							
7¼	Greenford					8	30		9	30			1248					2 47		4 14
	Marylebone ....dep.	156	106	357	108	4				10	6	10 35	1215		1255		1 37	1 52	2 10	2 30
	Wembley Hill	5	276	126	477	228	16				10	47		1	7			1 572	22	
	Sudbury & Harrow Rd.	5	316	166		517	268	20				10	53		1	11			2	12 29
	South Harrow	5	346	226		547	318	23				10	56		1	14			2	42 29
10¼	Northolt Junction		346	597	368	37				11	1			1	22			2	93 34
12	Ruislip and Ickenham	5	426	347		408	428	45			11	6		1	27			2	40
14½	Denham ‡	5	476	43		7	458	518			11	9			1	31			2	46
15½	Denham Golf Club Plat.			7	48				9	48		11	13			1	51			2	49
17½	Gerrard's Cross	5	536	517	137	53			9	51		1148		1	51	361	50			26 13
21½	Beaconsfield §	6	16	597	218	3			10	1		11	26		1	41	462	7		3
24¾	High Wycombe arr.	6	7	67	288	16			10	15	1135	11	35	1251	1	23	452	15		8
40	High Wycombe dep.	7	8	8	57		9	209	42		1014	1046	1253	1	36		2	17		
28¼	West Wycombe	7	10	8	8		9	159	41		1018	1050					2	20		
31½	Saunderton ‖ ..76, 690	7	16	8	8		9	52			1021	1054					2	31		
34¼	Princes Risboro' 46, arr.	7	39	9	14		9	589	47		1024	11	5		1	61	43	2	51		

Down. — Week Days—Continued.

Station	aft	aft	aft	aft	aft	aft	aft	aft	aft	aft	aft	aft
Paddington		4	40		5	23		6	25		6	57
Westbourne Park												
Acton *											6	59
Ealing (Broadway) †											6	12
West Ealing											6	16
Greenford							6	38			7	32
Marylebone ....dep.	4	36		4	50	5	356	406	47		7	358
Wembley Hill						5	466		6	47		7
Sudbury & Harrow Rd.						5	206	5	6	51		7
South Harrow						5	26	29	6	54		7
Northolt Junction						6	40	30		7	10	
Ruislip and Ickenham		5	20	5	5	196	35		6		7	157
Denham ‡		5	47		6	16		6	517	7		7
Denham Golf Club Plat.						6	537	10			c
Gerrard's Cross	5	865	225	516	5		6	587	157	777	317	55
Beaconsfield §		5	165	326	6	13		6	67	267	17	
High Wycombe arr.		5	295	396	1136	20		7	147	327	24	
40 High Wycombe dep.	5	7		5	245	396	113	29		7	15	
West Wycombe			5	476	18			7	17			
Saunderton ‖ ..76			5	566	23			7	24			
Princes Risboro' 46, arr.	5	19	5	265	586	29		7	29			

Down. — Sundays.

Station	mrn	mrn	mrn	mrn	mrn	aft	aft	aft	aft	aft	aft	aft
Paddington ....dep.	9	129	50		1110		1117		2	27		5
Westbourne Park							1119		2	25		5
Acton *							1125		2	32		5
Ealing (Broadway) †	9	21					1128		2	42	4	17
West Ealing	9	23					1132		2	45		7
Greenford	9	34					1139		2	51	4	25
Marylebone ....dep.	5	50				1115		2	25		4	30
Wembley Hill	9	2			1102		2					
Sudbury & Harrow Rd.	8				1103		2	30				
South Harrow	9	11			1104		2	34				
Northolt Junction	9	169	39		1054		2					
Ruislip and Ickenham	9	209	44		1054		1145	4:3				
Denham ‡	9	259	50		1055		1154	45				
Denham Golf Club Plat.	9	289	53		105		1157	2	50			
Gerrard's Cross	9	316	8		1113							
Beaconsfield §	9	4310	8		1113							
High Wycombe arr.	9	5610	1610	1056	1153							
40 High Wycombe dep.	9	5210	20		1121							
West Wycombe		9	5810	26		1127						
Saunderton ‖ .. 79, 694	10	410	33		1133							
Princes Risboro' 46, arr.	1010	1057			1139	1152						

NOTES.

A Slip Carriage.
a Stops to set down from London on informing the Guard at Marylebone.
b Stops to set down from London on informing the Guard at Paddington.
c Stops to set down.
e Stops to take up only.
i Call at Seer Green Halt (for Beaconsfield Golf Club), 6 minutes after leaving Gerrard's Cross.
W Stops on Saturdays only to set down from London on informing Guard the at Marylebone.
* About 1 mile from Churchfield Road Station.

† ¼ mile to North Ealing and 1¼ miles to South Ealing Stations, Metropolitan District.   ‡ Station for Harefield (1½ miles).   § Station for Penn (2¾ miles).   ‖ Station for Bradenham (1½ miles), Saunderton Village is 1 mile from Princes Risboro' Station.

LONDON, BRENTHAM, and GREENFORD (Motor Cars—One class only).—G. W.

Down. — Week Days.

Miles	Station	mrn	mrn	mrn	mrn	mrn	aft	aft	aft	aft	aft	aft	aft	aft	aft	aft	aft	aft
	Paddington ....dep.	7	127	408	489	301024	11501257	121	502	252	423	503	53	404	545	125	356	156	557
1¼	Westbourne Park ¶	7	207	483	569	48	11584	5	1	58		2	502	583	123	485	2		7
4¾	Park Royal	7	237	518	509	511034	12	1¾	81	222	13	222	533	13	165	515	55	225	456
5¼	Brentham, fr N. Ealing ¶	7	238	09	810	2104	212121	171	303	103	493	23	103	254	05	14	b	5	92
7¼	Greenford 42 arr.																		

Down. — Sundays.

Station	mrn	mrn	mrn	aft	aft	aft	aft	aft	aft	aft	aft	aft
Paddington ....dep.	9	3810	4012	412	402	102	463	153	404	626	26	507
Westbourne Park ¶	9	3610	4312	419	61	445	142	493	103	444	566	64
Park Royal	9	4710	52	1252	124	422	573	273	525	46	147	27
Brentham, fr N. Ealing ¶	9	5010	551	1351	2171	552	562	5	302	555	487	57
Greenford 42	9	5711	301	42	22	22	325	73	254	25	146	247

a Does not call at Old Oak Lane Halt.
b Runs to Drayton Green (Ealing).
E Except Saturdays.
S Saturdays only.
V Runs to West Ealing, see page 33.
¶ "Halts" at Old Oak Lane, between Westbourne Park and Park Royal, and Perivale, between Brentham and Greenford.

GERRARD'S CROSS, DENHAM, and UXBRIDGE (Motor Cars—One class only).—G.W.

Down. — Week Days only.

Miles	Station	mrn	mrn	mrn	mrn	aft	aft	aft	aft	aft	aft	aft
	Gerrard's Cross ....dep.	6	428	89	8	1027	1153	52	234	185	407	28	3510	0
1¼	Denham Golf Club Platform		8	129	121044	1191	92	274	225	44			
2¼	Denham			9	498	159	161044	13	1222	304	295	487	9	4510	7
3¼	Uxbridge (High Street) 53 arr.		9	588	249	211042	1211	213	324	345	577	188	5410	16

PADDINGTON

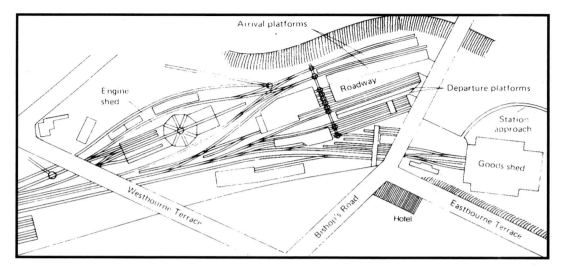

IV.   The first terminus was west of the present one, on the site of the later goods depot. The lines are connected by wagon turntables, which were mainly used for flat wagons for the conveyance of the horse-drawn carriages of the gentry. Hence the four short sidings ending at a dock on the roadway.

1.   The arches under Bishops Road (right) were used for parcels, waiting rooms and offices. After 1854 they carried the tracks to the new terminus. The departure building is behind the bus, and the tall building on the left housed coaches on the ground floor. Intending passengers walked through the arch graced with a canopy. (Illustrated London News)

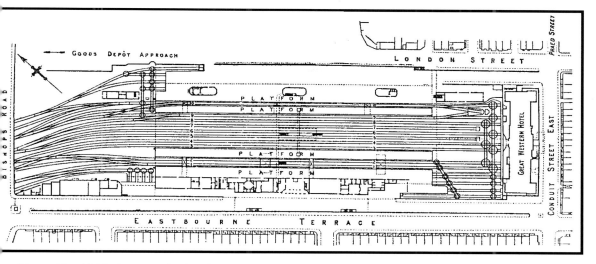

V.   The 1854 plan reveals that there were ten tracks, but only five platforms. The hotel (right) had an exclusive footbridge leading to all of them. Wagon turntables proliferated, but they lasted only until about 1870.

2.   The end of the 1854 roof spans are evident, together with the covered footway to the Bishops Road station used by Hammersmith & City trains. No. 3241 was one of a batch of 2-4-0s built at Swindon in 1892, the year in which the last broad gauge train left this station. (Lens of Sutton)

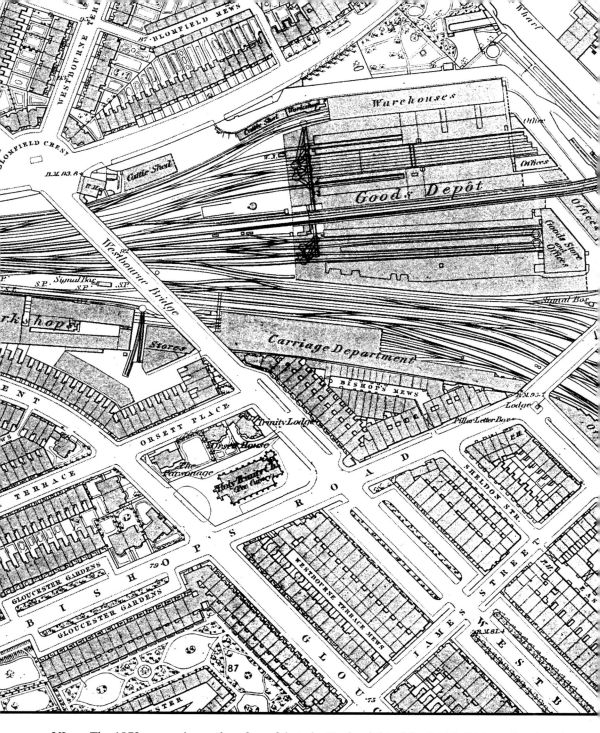

VI.   The 1872 survey is worthy of careful study. To the right of the fold is Bishops Road station which opened on 10th January 1863 and was used by GWR trains to and from the City. Above it is the coal depot and the sidings on the canal wharf. At the bottom of the right page is the MR's Praed Street station, which came into use on 1st October 1868 and is now on the Circle Line.

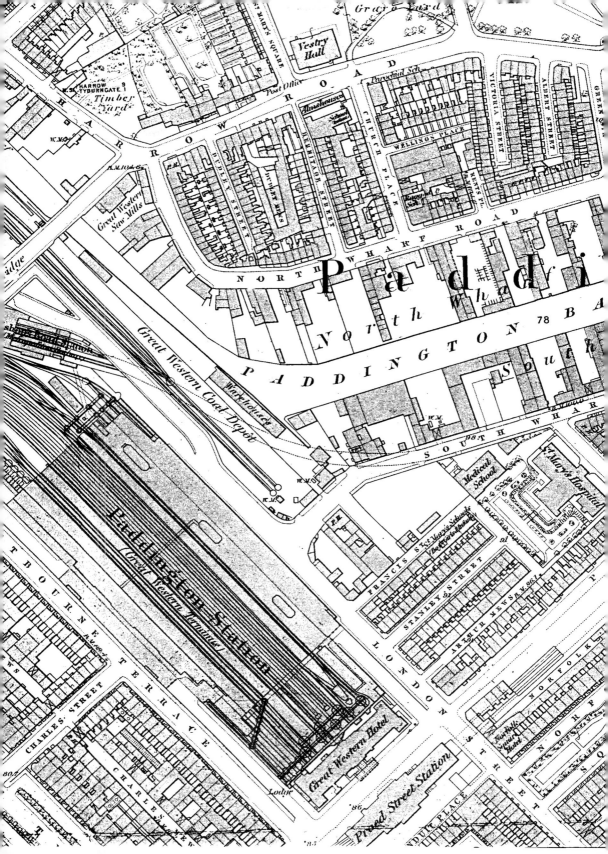

3.   The Great Western Hotel (right) opened on 9th June 1854. Centre is the end of the main roof and on the left is the GWR head office and the canopy over the main entrance. (Lens of Sutton)

4.   The 8.30am from Birkenhead is arriving on 27th August 1910, soon after Bishops Road bridge had lost its brick arches in favour of a lattice steel structure. On the right is the Departure Box, which was in use until 2nd July 1933, when colour light signals arrived. No. 102 was a 4-4-2 purchased by the GWR in 1903. It was a De Glehn 4 cylinder compound used to compare performance with existing 2 cylinder engines. (K.Nunn/LCGB)

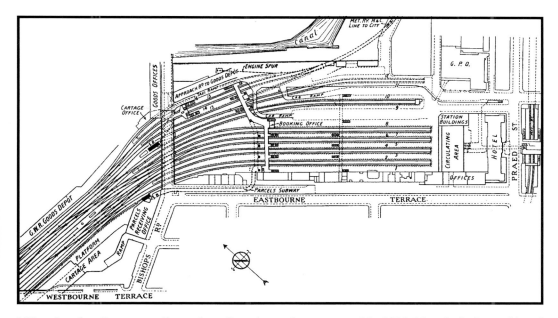

VII.   London Street was diverted to allow the station to expand in 1909-15 and platforms 11 and 12 were built under the diverted street. Further changes in 1930-33 resulted in the layout shown. The Bishops Road station was redesignated "Paddington Suburban" on 10th September 1933 and the platforms numbered 13 to 16. The engine spur was used by electric locomotives taking GWR trains to the City, a practice that ceased on 25th September 1939. (Railway Magazine)

5.   No. 6005 *King George II* is approaching the terminus with an excursion on 1st March 1959 and is passing the massive goods depot which was rebuilt in 1925-26, closed in 1975 and demolished in 1986. The circular signals remained until November 1967 when most local signal boxes were closed in favour of a panel box at Old Oak Common. (B.W.Leslie)

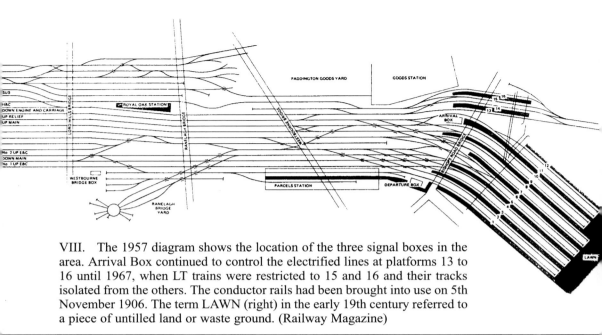

VIII. The 1957 diagram shows the location of the three signal boxes in the area. Arrival Box continued to control the electrified lines at platforms 13 to 16 until 1967, when LT trains were restricted to 15 and 16 and their tracks isolated from the others. The conductor rails had been brought into use on 5th November 1906. The term LAWN (right) in the early 19th century referred to a piece of untilled land or waste ground. (Railway Magazine)

6.   In Network SouthEast livery, no. 47709 drifts past the former parcels depot on 13th March 1991 with the 06.39 from Banbury. Work started in 1992 to relay and rearrange all this trackwork to give six bidirectional lines. (M.J.Stretton)

7.   This panorama towards the buffers is from 14th September 1996 and includes Thames Turbo no. 165106. All was about to change again; platforms 6 and 7 were widened in readiness for the Heathrow Express which started a limited service on 19th January 1998. Overhead wires were provided at platforms 1 to 11 and platform widths were altered. (P.G.Barnes)

Our *Paddington to Ealing* album contains 39 photographs of Paddington and more detailed explanations of the alterations at this fascinating historic site.

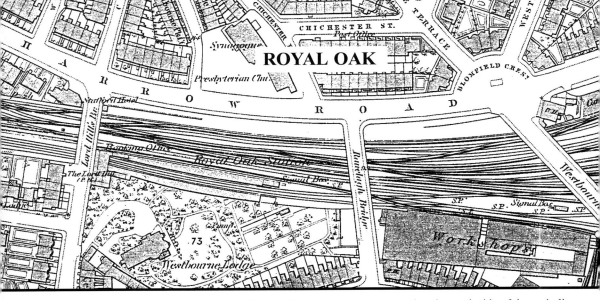

IX.   Reference to the last diagram will show that the station was moved to the north side of the main lines. This took place in 1878 when a subway for Hammersmith trains was provided. This 1872 survey overlaps map VI and reveals the original position of the station, close to a spacious mansion in parkland. The station opened on 30th October 1871. GWR trains ceased to call at Royal Oak on 1st October 1934 and the station became LT property on 1st January 1970. Paddington had a small generator installed for electric lighting in 1880. The second one was put in the workshops on the right in 1886 and it ran until 1907, despite complaints from the neighbours.

8.   A westward view from the London Transport island platform on 18th July 1987 includes Lord Hill's Bridge, one of many rebuilt in about 1909. A single and a 2-car DMU largely obscure the three carriage sidings and the pilot siding. (P.G.Barnes)

WESTBOURNE PARK

9.　　Recorded from the end of the platform on 30th September 1948 was no. 6925 *Hackness Hall* with the 9.25am from Princes Risborough on the up relief line. The other train is on the up main; the goods lines are on the right. (S.C.Nash)

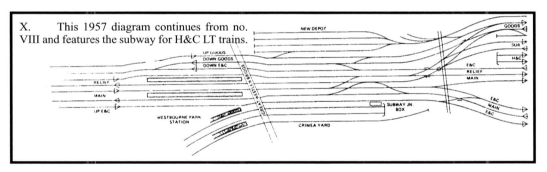

X.　　This 1957 diagram continues from no. VIII and features the subway for H&C LT trains.

10.　　The subway is seen from the brake van of an Acton-Smithfield meat train in 1956. The line on which it is travelling was taken out of use in the following year and the service was discontinued on 30th July 1962, ending steam on the Circle Line. The diesel parcels van was nearing the end of its life as well. (V.Mitchell)

XI. The Hammersmith branch is the lower line on the left of this 1872 map. It opened on 13th June 1864 and also carried passenger trains to Kensington (Addison Road) on the West London Line from July 1864 to October 1940. Westbourne Park opened on 1st February 1866 and had the suffix "& Kensal Green" until 1st November 1871, when platforms were added on the main line. The engine shed at Paddington was closed on 2nd March 1852 and replaced by larger premises here. Further capacity was added in 1862 and in 1873. Closure followed on 18th March 1906, when even larger facilities were completed at Old Oak Common. The former depot area was dedicated to goods traffic to supplement the yard shown to the south of the main line. Freight facilities were withdrawn on 17th July 1967.

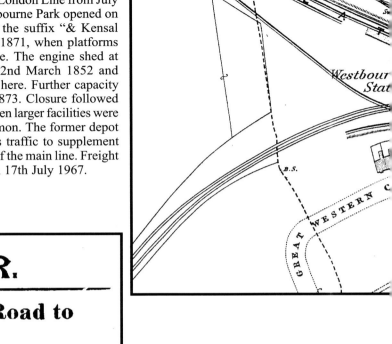

244

C.R.

Bodmin Road to

Westbourne Park

Cornwall Railway luggage label

11. The 1871 platforms were photographed almost a century after construction, by which time they were little used. They were closed on 14th March 1992, the final down timetable showing a regular hourly train to Greenford via Ealing, weekdays only. (Lens of Sutton)

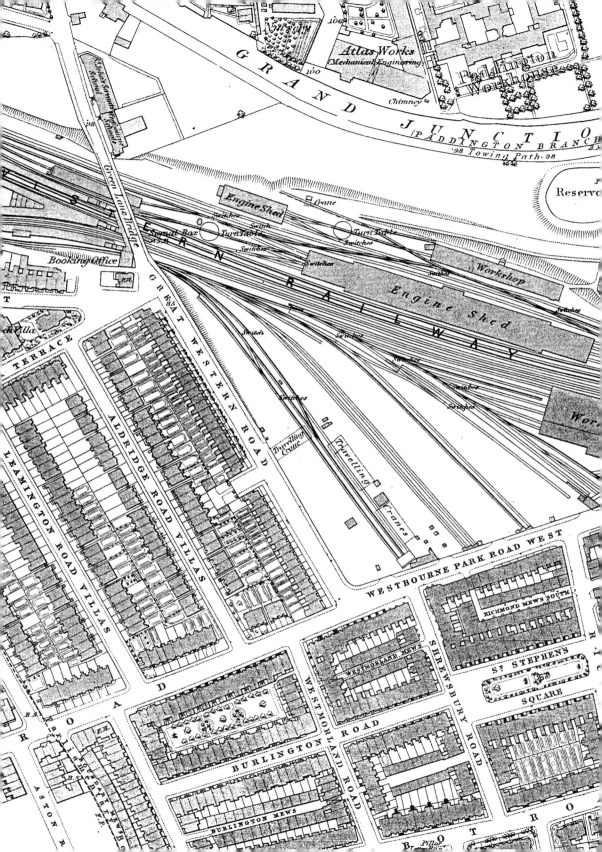

12.   The platforms were removed within a week of closure, as a sewer needed alterations prior to track lowering to give clearance under the bridge for 25kV wires. The white panel was erected at the top of the stairs to the relief line platforms, prior to their removal. No. L263 was being used as a route learning special on 20th December 1992. (S.P.Derek)

WEST OF WESTBOURNE PARK

XII.   This 1870 map showing double track and a short siding makes an interesting comparison with no. XV in *Paddington to Ealing*. This is the site of the Ladbroke Grove disaster on 5th October 1999; the road on the bridge had been thus renamed long before then.

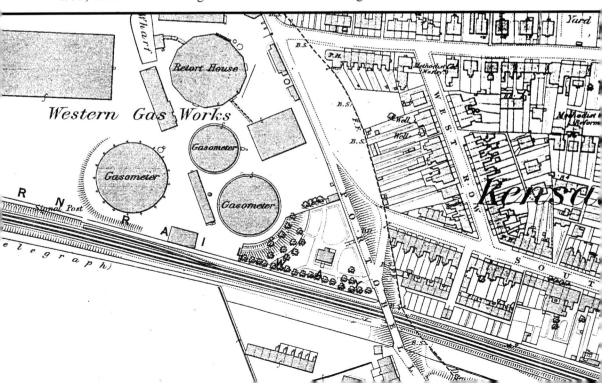

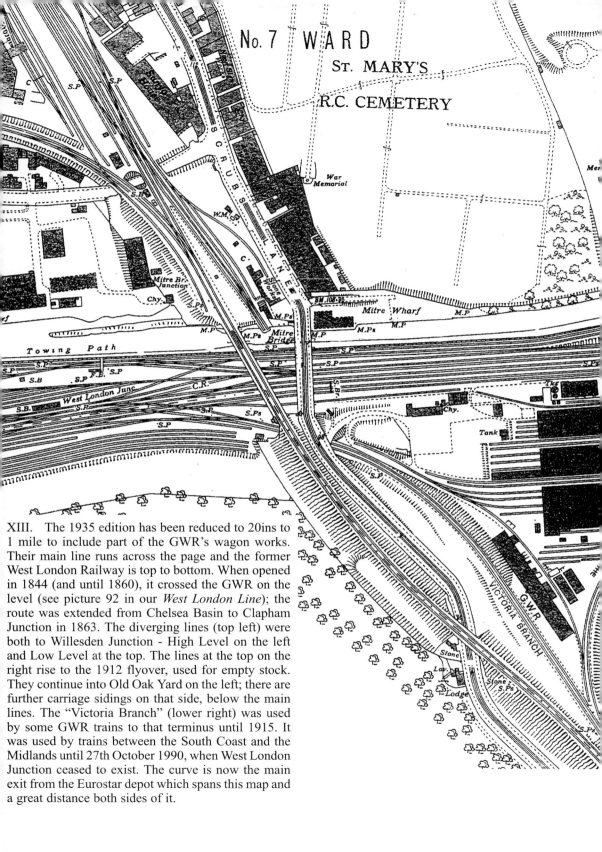

No. 7 WARD

St. MARY'S

R.C. CEMETERY

War Memorial

Mitre Wharf

Mitre Bridge

Towing Path

West London Junc.

VICTORIA BRANCH

G.W.R.

Lodge

Tank

XIII.   The 1935 edition has been reduced to 20ins to 1 mile to include part of the GWR's wagon works. Their main line runs across the page and the former West London Railway is top to bottom. When opened in 1844 (and until 1860), it crossed the GWR on the level (see picture 92 in our *West London Line*); the route was extended from Chelsea Basin to Clapham Junction in 1863. The diverging lines (top left) were both to Willesden Junction - High Level on the left and Low Level at the top. The lines at the top on the right rise to the 1912 flyover, used for empty stock. They continue into Old Oak Yard on the left; there are further carriage sidings on that side, below the main lines. The "Victoria Branch" (lower right) was used by some GWR trains to that terminus until 1915. It was used by trains between the South Coast and the Midlands until 27th October 1990, when West London Junction ceased to exist. The curve is now the main exit from the Eurostar depot which spans this map and a great distance both sides of it.

OLD OAK COMMON

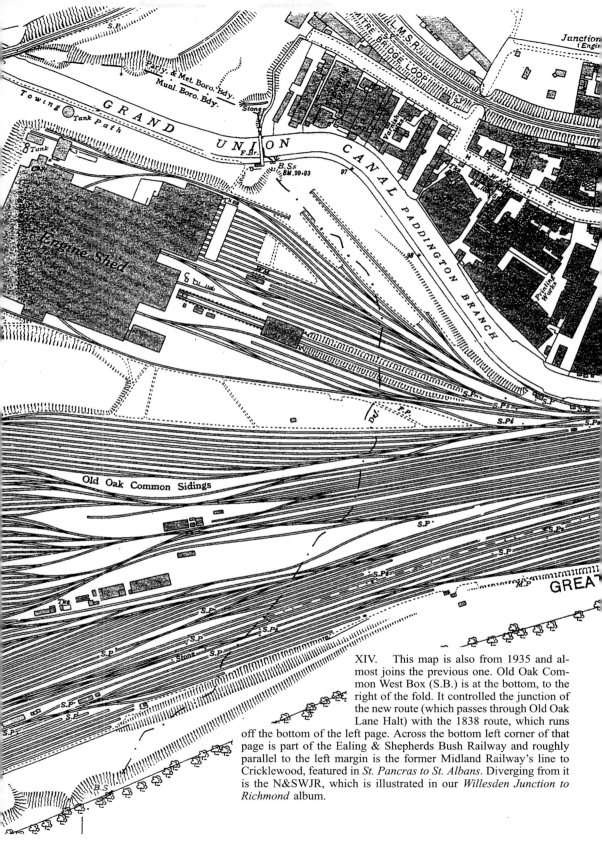

S.P.

Parly. & Met. Boro. Bdy.

Munl. Boro. Bdy.

T O W I N G   G R A N D

Tank Path

Stone

U N I O N

F.Br.

B.Ss
BM.99·93

97

Tank

S.P.

Engine Shed

L.M.S.R.

MITRE BRIDGE LOOP

Junction
(Engin

Various
Bridge

C A N A L   P A D D I N G T O N   B R A N C H

Printing
Works

Def.

F.P.

Old Oak Common Sidings

S.P.

S.P·

S.P.

S.Ps

S.Ps

S.P.

S.P·

S.P.

S.Ps

S.Ps

Stone

Tks

M.P.

GREAT

S.P·

S.P.

S.P.

S.P.

S.P.

B.S.

XIV. This map is also from 1935 and almost joins the previous one. Old Oak Common West Box (S.B.) is at the bottom, to the
right of the fold. It controlled the junction of
the new route (which passes through Old Oak
Lane Halt) with the 1838 route, which runs
off the bottom of the left page. Across the bottom left corner of that
page is part of the Ealing & Shepherds Bush Railway and roughly
parallel to the left margin is the former Midland Railway's line to
Cricklewood, featured in *St. Pancras to St. Albans*. Diverging from it
is the N&SWJR, which is illustrated in our *Willesden Junction to
Richmond* album.

13.   Four sheds, each with a central turntable, provided 112 roads and housed locomotives from 1906 to 1965. About 500 tons of coal were consumed daily for most of its life and the repair shed was adjacent, on the north side. The turntable was fully boarded and is in the foreground of this photo from the 1930s. (LPC/NRM)

14.   The rare open days have been extremely popular. No. 5051 *Drysllwyn Castle* was working a shuttle service to Paddington on 20th September 1981. The photograph is included to emphasise the great extent of the depot, the buildings on the left having been added in 1976 for the servicing of HSTs. Further views can be found in pictures 85 to 97 in our *Paddington to Ealing* album. (F.Hornby)

OLD OAK LANE HALT

15. The halt opened on 1st October 1906 when the route beyond Greenford was completed. It was closed temporarily from 1st February 1915 to 29th March 1920. The bay platform was in use from 20th June 1932 to 2nd June 1940. The outline of Old Oak Common West Box is in the background and the main line is on the right. (Stations UK)

16. No. 5410 is propelling autocoach no. 198 which is forming the 6.3pm Greenford to Westbourne Park service on 24th June 1947. The halt closed six days later as autotrains were withdrawn following completion of the Central Line. The letters A to E were displayed on the five similar trains. The water column was provided for those terminating here. (H.C.Casserley)

17.   The halt was just beyond the bridge which carries the Willesden Junction to Richmond line and no. 46521 will have just passed its site on 29th December 1994 while working a "Mince Pie Special" from Paddington and back via the Greenford Loop. The route had been singled from Old Oak Reception Line 1 to Royal Oak in July 1993. On the right is the former Ealing & Shepherds Bush Railway. The parallel double track had been to the left of it until 9th March 1964. (S.P.Derek)

NORTH ACTON

XV.   This 1935 map overlaps the previous one and shows a small signal box near the points to the halt bay. Operationally it was only a ground frame.

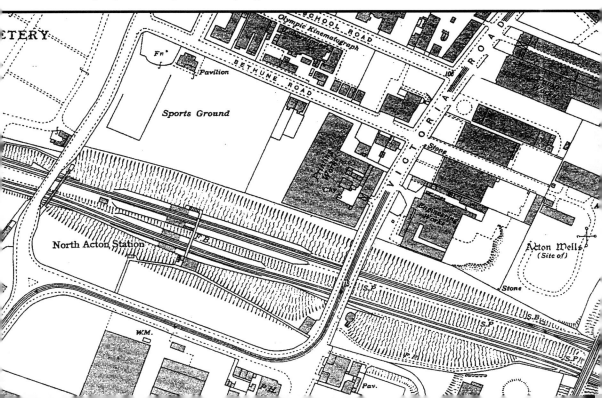

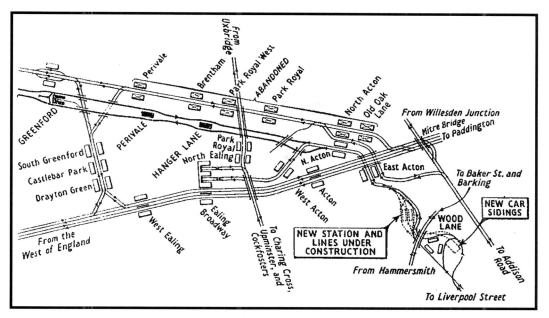

XVI. A 1947 diagram shows the Central Line extension with a thicker line and a bracket around the GWR stations abandoned. (Railway Magazine)

18. An autotrain bound for Greenford leaves the wooden platform on 29th June 1947. The goods lines from Ealing, added in 1938, are to the left of it. The station opened on 5th November 1923; North Acton Halt had been in the distance until 1st February 1913. It had two short platforms, on the GWR lines only. (S.C.Nash)

19. Seen on the same day is 0-6-0PT no. 5417 with the 5.58pm Old Oak Lane to Northolt service. The sign on the left carried the words CHANGE FOR ELECTRIC TRAINS TO WEST END & CITY. Most passengers did so, thus there was little point in running the local steam trains much further. Note the goods train running between Willesden Junction and Acton Central. (H.C.Casserley)

20.   A trolleybus proceeds to Harlesden as a Central Line train departs east in about 1960. The footbridge had been reduced in length, but all the GWR-built buildings remained. The footpath access is evident. The left platform became an island on 22nd March 1993, when a third track was laid. The centre one became reversible. (T.Wright)

WEST OF NORTH ACTON

21.   North Acton Junction Box opened on 3rd August 1920 and is seen in this and the next picture soon afterwards. Here we see a Central London train from Ealing Broadway. North Acton Halt had been in the right foreground until 1913, but was in the way of the Ealing & Shepherds Bush Railway (left), which eventually opened for freight in 1917. (E.Course coll.)

22.   A view towards London includes one of the GWR's experimental three-position semaphores in the off position giving a green aspect. At 45 degrees, a yellow light was shown. It is seen close to the train in the previous picture. When six parallel tracks were provided in 1938, the points to the new pair were further east and there was no connection to the LT tracks. A new box with 32 levers was built in 1940 and this lasted until 2nd December 1966. (J.Scott-Morgan coll./R.S.Carpenter)

23.   The new box was photographed on 24th August 1957, along with the 1946 bridge which allowed trains to West Ruislip (one is illustrated) to pass under the Ealing Broadway lines. The white twin-arch bridge carried a siding to four different firms. More private sidings diverge on the right; see the map after next, right page. The siding on the right was the only one remaining in use in 2002, it carrying Marcon aggregates. (A.A.Jackson)

PARK ROYAL

XVII.   The Royal Agricultural Society decided that it should have a permanent showground and purchased from Twyford Abbey (top) a large part of its park. Combining two words, it became Park Royal. The 1912 edition at 6ins to 1 mile shows in black the roofs on the station buildings and both footbridges. The station and goods yard were opened temporarily in 1903 for the first show, regular services starting on 1st May 1904. The show that year, like the first, was a financial failure and the land was sold off to industry. However, the football ground was a success and long trains called on some Saturdays. It was used by Queens Park Rangers until 1915. Lower right is the 1907 power station which supplied Paddington (and other stations), Old Oak Common and also traction current for the trains on the joint lines between Ealing and Shepherds Bush (Wood Lane) and between Hammersmith and Paddington.

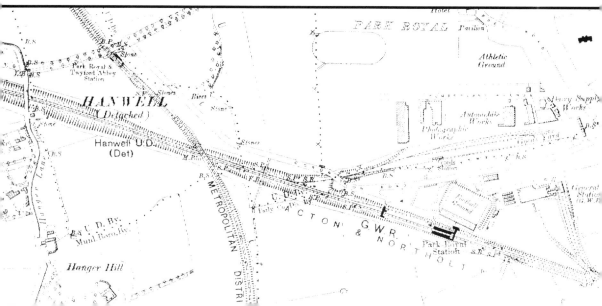

24.   A railmotor stands at the up platform which could accommodate passenger trains on both sides for some years. The short-lived western footbridge is in the background of this indifferent postcard. (E.Course coll.)

25.   The sidings were provided initially for the showground, but a conventional goods yard was soon established to serve local industry. The goods shed is seen in April 1936; a crane was listed as of six-ton capacity in 1938, but the one shown was rated at 30cwt. (NRM)

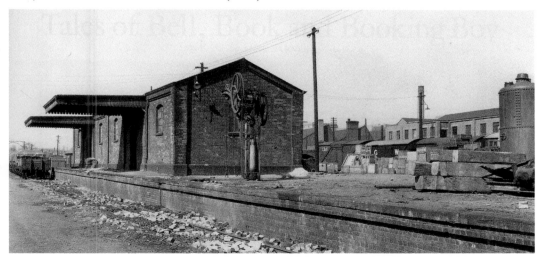

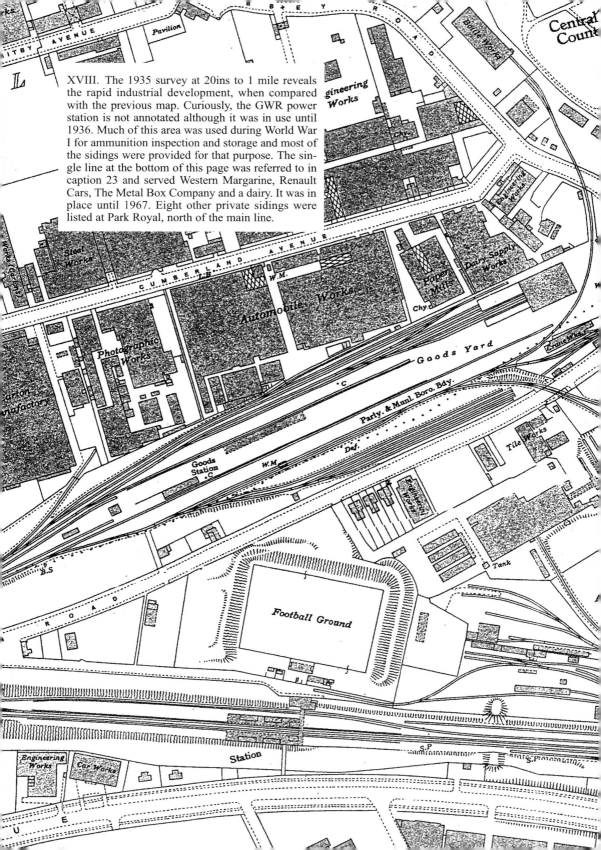

XVIII. The 1935 survey at 20ins to 1 mile reveals the rapid industrial development, when compared with the previous map. Curiously, the GWR power station is not annotated although it was in use until 1936. Much of this area was used during World War I for ammunition inspection and storage and most of the sidings were provided for that purpose. The single line at the bottom of this page was referred to in caption 23 and served Western Margarine, Renault Cars, The Metal Box Company and a dairy. It was in place until 1967. Eight other private sidings were listed at Park Royal, north of the main line.

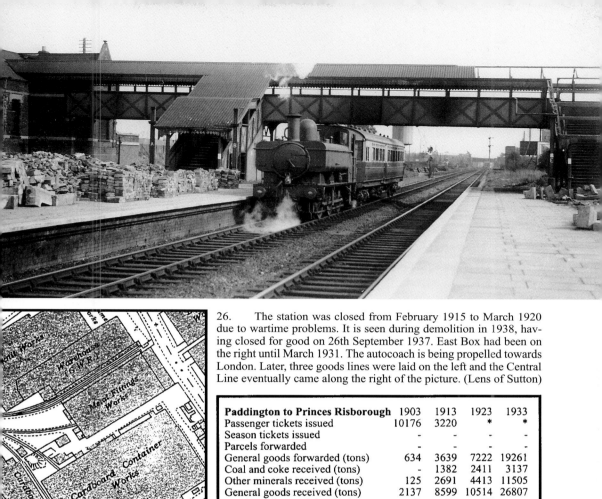

26.　　The station was closed from February 1915 to March 1920 due to wartime problems. It is seen during demolition in 1938, having closed for good on 26th September 1937. East Box had been on the right until March 1931. The autocoach is being propelled towards London. Later, three goods lines were laid on the left and the Central Line eventually came along the right of the picture. (Lens of Sutton)

Paddington to Princes Risborough	1903	1913	1923	1933
Passenger tickets issued	10176	3220	*	*
Season tickets issued	-	-	-	-
Parcels forwarded	-	-	-	-
General goods forwarded (tons)	634	3639	7222	19261
Coal and coke received (tons)	-	1382	2411	3137
Other minerals received (tons)	125	2691	4413	11505
General goods received (tons)	2137	8599	10514	26807
Trucks of livestock handled	63	77	27	-

(* not available.)

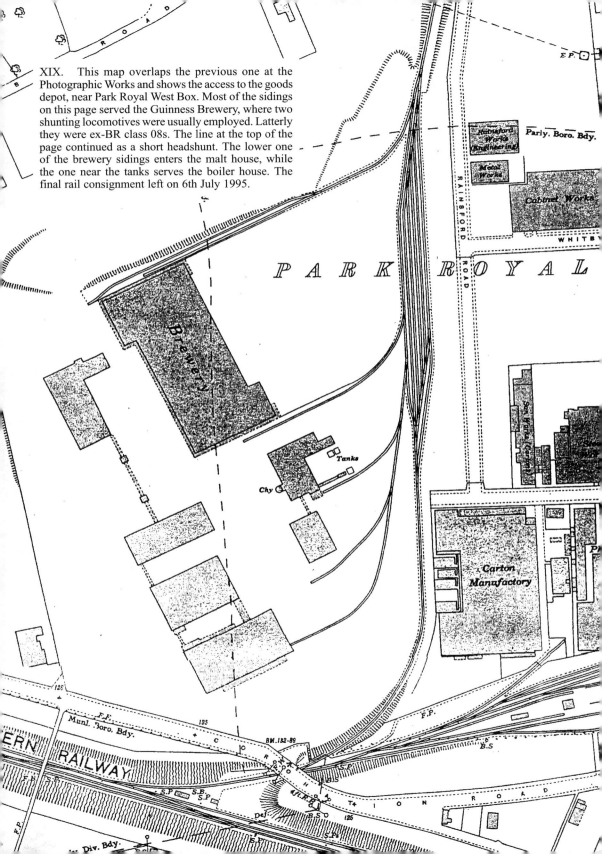

XIX.   This map overlaps the previous one at the Photographic Works and shows the access to the goods depot, near Park Royal West Box. Most of the sidings on this page served the Guinness Brewery, where two shunting locomotives were usually employed. Latterly they were ex-BR class 08s. The line at the top of the page continued as a short headshunt. The lower one of the brewery sidings enters the malt house, while the one near the tanks serves the boiler house. The final rail consignment left on 6th July 1995.

Rainsford Works Rodliner ink

Parly. Boro. Bdy.

Metal Works

Cabinet Works

WHITE

RAINSFORD ROAD

P A R K   R O Y A L

E P

Brewery

Tanks

Chy

Carton Manufactory

125

135

F.P.

Munl. Boro. Bdy.

BM.132·89

RAILWAY

S.P.

S.B.

S.P.

B.S

F.P.

B.S

S.P.

T+I O N   R O A D

De J.

B.S

125

Div. Bdy.

S.Ps

27.   Park Royal West Box and the Coronation Road bridge over the line to the goods yard are featured, as is the Royal Agricultural Society's "permanent" headquarters, which proved to be so shortlived: 1903-04. The box had 55 levers. (*Acton* - published 1912)

28.   The station had been in the right background of this June 1979 view. Part of the goods yard was used as a Freightliner terminal from 1968 to 1982. The box was simply "Park Royal" after 1931 and remained in use until 15th July 1979, when a ground frame was provided. (Brunel University/Wookey coll.)

29.   A "King" class 4-6-0 speeds towards London with an express from Birmingham in May 1962 and passes under the Piccadilly Line. Map XVII shows this as Metropolitan District Railway in 1912. This picture was taken from the same footbridge as the previous two, but from its west side. The platforms of Park Royal West had been each side of the rear coaches between 20th June 1932 and 15th June 1947. The siding on the right ended just beyond the bridge and was a continuation of the one on the left of picture 28. (T.Wright)

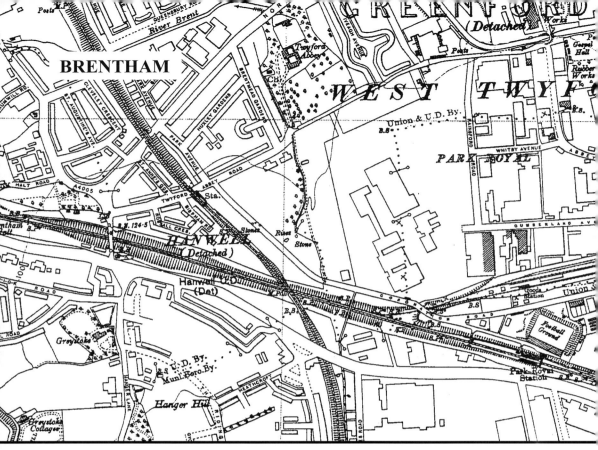

XX.   The 1919 revision shows the "halt" near the left border. It opened on 1st May 1911, following the closure of Twyford Abbey Halt, which had been subjected to a landslide as it was in the deep cutting, to the left of the bridge, at the southern end of the then new North Circular Road (top). The still winding rural Hanger Lane is lower left; a Central Line station of that name was built in 1946, adjacent to the site of Twyford Abbey Halt.

30. Twyford Abbey Halt and its inclined footways are recorded in this westward view. It was in an area of rapidly developing "high-class housing". (E.Course coll.)

31.   No. 6026 *King John* heads the 7.10pm Paddington to Shrewsbury on 16th June 1938. The rear of the train is close to the site of Twyford Abbey Halt and the bridge for the North Circular Road. On the right is the modern Western Avenue and site preparation for the Central Line. The train will soon cross the 122yd long Brent Viaduct. (K.Nunn/LCGB)

PERIVALE HALT

32.   The term "halt" was used inconsistently on this route, but there were certainly few folk to use the trains here in the early years. This view of the fields is towards London. (Lens of Sutton)

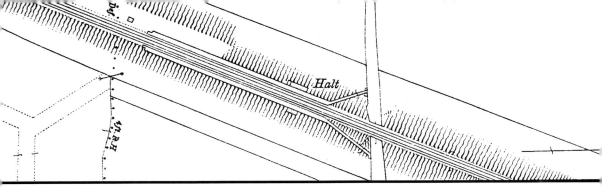

XXI. The 1913 map shows the outline of some roads awaiting houses. Sidings were later provided on the north side for Sandersons (wallpaper), Bulmer (cider) and Electro-Metallic Recovery (detinning). The signal box had 13 levers and was in use until 14th September 1955.

33.   The halt was in use from 1st May 1904 to 15th June 1947, although closed temporarily in 1915-20. Preparatory work for the Central Line is in progress on the left; the new station was built behind the camera. (Lens of Sutton)

EAST OF GREENFORD

XXII. The diagram shows the layout since East Curve was singled in June 1970 and the main line to Northolt Junction from West Junction was singled on 29th May 1990. East Station Box (near West Junction) remains in use, East Loop Box and South Junction Box having closed on 8th December 1956.

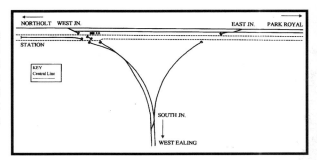

34.   No. 6024 *King Edward I* proceeds cautiously off the Greenford Branch on 21st March 1993 with the 10.20 Ealing Broadway to Stratford-upon-Avon Mothering Sunday "William Shakespeare Express". The locomotive bears the "Cambrian Coast Express" headboard. Starting from Ealing Broadway due to major track remodelling at Paddington, the train is joining the main line at Greenford West Junction, passing the 76-lever signal box known as Greenford East, which controlled some of the last remaining semaphore signalling in the London area. This was the penultimate steam working over the Chiltern Line, the special steam programme being curtailed for 'operational reasons'. The sidings on the left had been used by Rockware Glass until about 1989 and thereafter by the signal engineers. (S.P.Derek)

35.   A few minutes later, Turbo no. 165132 working the 10.10 Paddington to West Ruislip hourly shuttle (arranged owing to the track remodelling at Paddington) comes off the Greenford branch at Greenford West Junction. It is running from the down line onto the bidirectional single line leading to Northolt Junction. The starter signal arm for the Greenford bay platform can be discerned above the rear driving cab. (S.P.Derek)

GREENFORD

XXIII. The 1913 survey shows the small goods yard from which a line leads to the extensive sidings of Pauling & Company. The land between these and the canal (left) was developed by J.Lyons in 1920.

G. W. R.

S.P. · Cr W.M. Cr Goods Shed

M.P. S.B. S.Ps

& N O R T H O L T

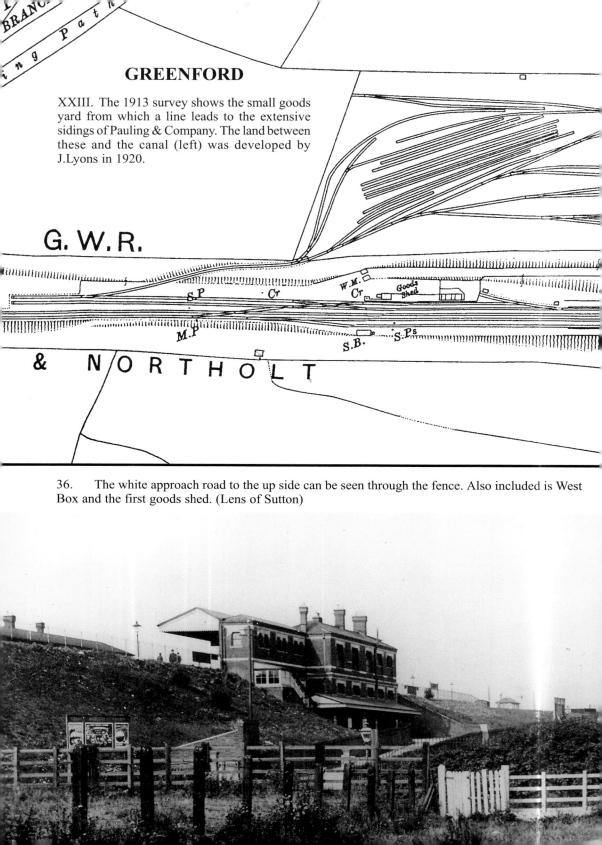

36. The white approach road to the up side can be seen through the fence. Also included is West Box and the first goods shed. (Lens of Sutton)

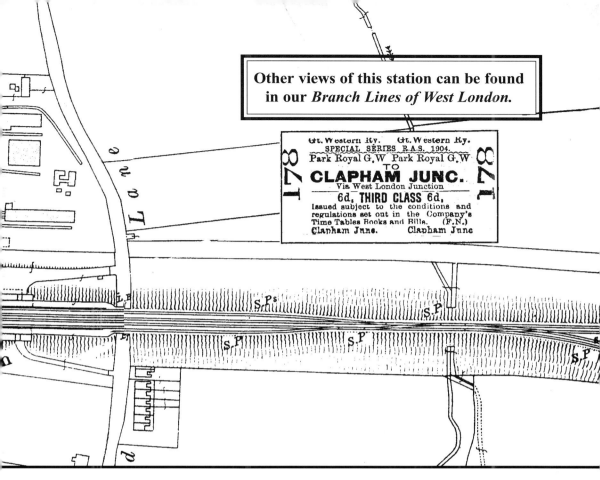

Other views of this station can be found in our *Branch Lines of West London*.

Gt. Western Ry.   Gt. Western Ry.
SPECIAL SERIES R.A.S. 1904.
Park Royal G.W   Park Royal G.W
TO
CLAPHAM JUNC.
Via West London Junction
6d, THIRD CLASS 6d,
Issued subject to the conditions and
regulations set out in the Company's
Time Tables Books and Bills.   (F.N.)
Clapham Junc.   Clapham Junc

37.   The once famous catering firm had four parallel sidings on the south side of their works, one of which (right) was under cover. This one continued west and had a branch parallel to the canal. One of the firm's locomotives is seen, the 1888 0-6-0ST *Tyersall*. Adjacent to it is the 1920 Sentinel no. 3143 *Stella*, one of the large fleet of modern vehicles with efficient water tube boilers, the inner half of which was easily dropped into a pit for servicing. (J.Lyons)

38.	The company was proud of its integrated transport policy, years ahead of its time but killed off by ignorant politicians. This picture was posed on the nearby Brentford branch at a location shown in picture 29 in our *Branch Lines of West London*. Their Greenford sidings were used until 1970. (J.Lyons)

39.	There was quadruple track through the station area from the outset and the associated two platforms remained in use until 17th June 1963 when almost all local trains were transferred to Marylebone. In the background is the station built for the Central Line extension in 1947; it included a centre bay platform for the Ealing Broadway autotrain and an escalator up to the platform. Ex-LBSCR no. 32425 *Trevose Head* is working the "Riverside Special" on 29th July 1956. (H.Davies)

40.   A westward view from the up platform shortly before its closure includes cement wagons near the larger 1932 goods shed and the 37-lever Station West Box, which closed on 8th August 1971. Behind it, the Central Line rises to a bridge over a line that was added in about 1928 to serve a variety of industrial premises. (B.W.Leslie)

41.   The bay came into use on 21st November 1948 and is seen on 14th June 1952 as 0-6-0PT no. 5420 propels autocoach no. 220 towards Ealing Broadway at 1.33pm. The Central Line flyovers are in the left background. (H.C.Casserley)

42.   Seen from the same point exactly six years later is no. 5012 *Berry Pomeroy Castle* with the 11.30am from Oxford to Paddington. The loop lines became sidings and the goods yard became a cement depot, after closure on 23rd May 1980. The staff increased from 14 in 1913 to 65 in 1938. (H.C.Casserley)

43.   The Ealing shuttle service from the bay was extended to Paddington in May 1988. Single railcars were generally used, this example being photographed on 15th December 1988, when in NSE livery. The station was built by the GWR and became LT property on 1st January 1948. (T.Wright)

NORTHOLT

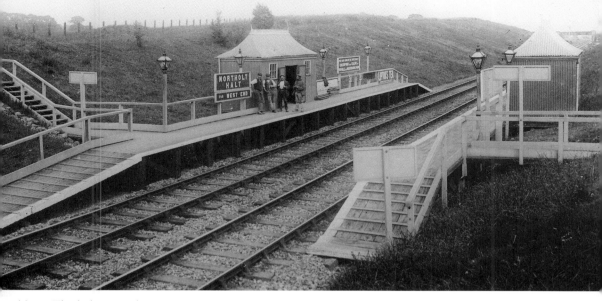

44.   The halt opened on 1st May 1907 and became a station on 23rd September 1929, when the platforms were lengthened. It justified five men by 1938. An aerodrome was opened nearby in 1915 and was used as a civil airport from 1946 to 1954. A racecourse opened in 1929 and generated some extra traffic. (Lens of Sutton)

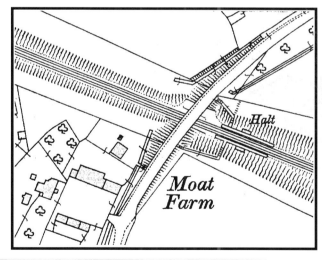

XXIV. The 1913 edition shows fields predominating. An up loop siding, with goods dock, and a 30-lever signal box were added west of the bridge in 1929. A down loop followed in 1932, mainly for the use of terminating autotrains.

45.   The down loop was removed to permit construction of the Central Line station, seen in the Summer of 1948. Autotrains continued to use the up loop between trips until the LT station came into use on 21st November 1948. The remaining loop became a siding and freight facilities were withdrawn on 1st September 1952. (NRM)

SOUTH RUISLIP

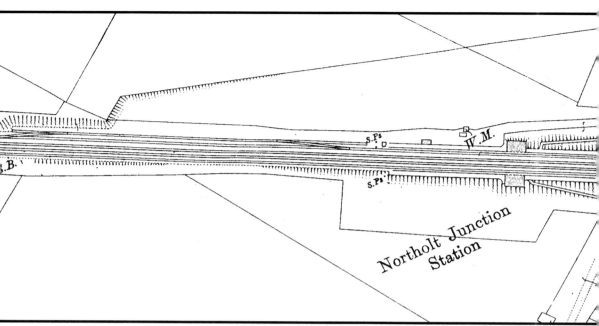

XXV. The Marylebone lines are shown each side of the Paddington ones, with East Junction Box in the middle. The name shown was changed to "South Ruislip & Northolt Junction" on 12th September 1932 and the suffix was dropped in October 1947. The single siding shown on this 1913 survey had a private branch from World War I to about 1958, plus a short dairy siding from 1959 to 1972.

46. The track on the right was removed in 1973 and the platform widened. An island platform was built for the Central Line and all were connected by a subway in 1948, but the new entrance building was not completed until 1961. Eight or nine men were employed here in the 1930s. (Lens of Sutton)

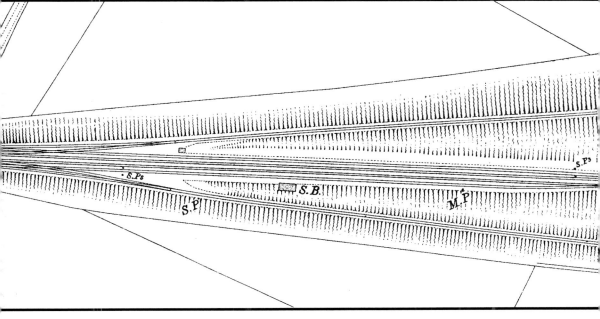

47.   The single siding is evident at the end of the up platform and the original entrance gate is on the right. Steps were provided at the London end of the platform in 1948. (R.S.Carpenter)

48.   A September 1969 view includes the signal box, which was designated "West" until "East" (see map) was closed on 17th July 1966. They had 55 and 29 levers respectively. The box seen lasted until 29th May 1990, when the route to Greenford was singled. (B.W.Leslie)

49.   No. 7029 *Clun Castle* proceeds cautiously over the junction while on clearance trials between Marylebone and Banbury on 18th May 1986. The track curving down to the right, then left under the Paddington lines, is the route from Marylebone. A siding was put in opposite the signal box in 1980 to serve a GLC Waste Transfer Depot. West Waste were despatching two trains of rubbish containers daily to Calvert in 2002. (S.P.Derek)

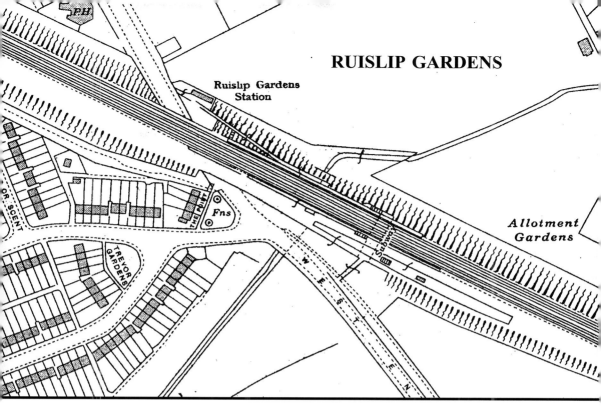

RUISLIP GARDENS

Ruislip Gardens
Station

Allotment
Gardens

XXVI. The 1940 edition reveals that the island platform for LT trains had been completed, although it would be another eight years before it could be used.

50.   The main line platforms were in use from 16th July 1934 until 21st July 1958. Quadruple track was provided from Northolt Junction to West Ruislip in 1906, to allow fast trains to overtake slow ones. (Lens of Sutton)

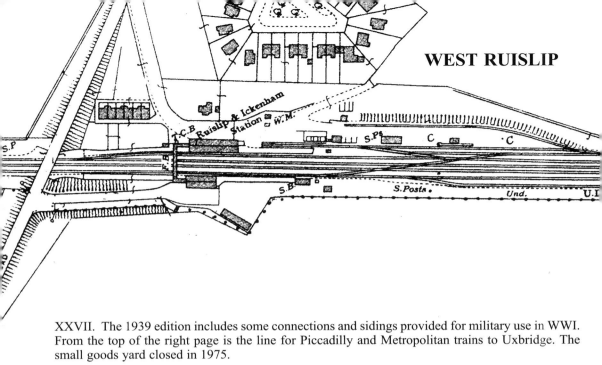

WEST RUISLIP

XXVII. The 1939 edition includes some connections and sidings provided for military use in WWI. From the top of the right page is the line for Piccadilly and Metropolitan trains to Uxbridge. The small goods yard closed in 1975.

51.   This postcard view includes the steeply inclined roadway to the down side (right), the original footbridge and railway houses, the large one being for the station master. The staff increased from 6 initially to 21 in 1938. (Lens of Sutton)

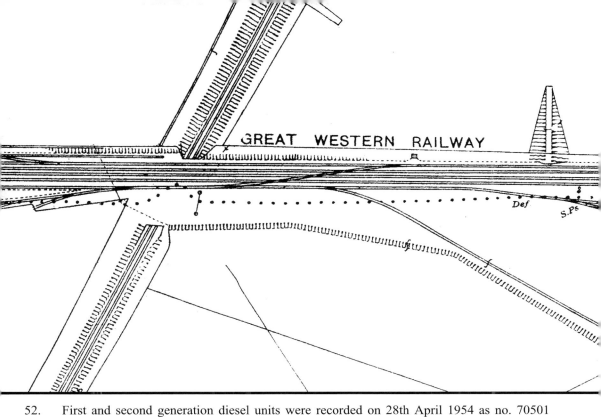

GREAT WESTERN RAILWAY

52.   First and second generation diesel units were recorded on 28th April 1954 as no. 70501 embarked on a trial run to Marylebone. No. W34W was one of the GWR's two parcels railcars. (K.Nunn/LCGB)

53.　　Two photographs from 14th June 1958 feature the new footbridge, which adjoined a new road-level booking hall built for the opening of the Central Line. A train of ex-LNER stock from Marylebone stands at the down platform, while a horsebox is on the right. The original up building was still standing in 2002. (H.C.Casserley)

54.　　The 11.30 Oxford to Paddington runs in behind no. 5012 *Berry Pomeroy Castle*. For many years, this was the only Paddington train to call here. The use of concrete and flat roofs gave an unimpressive result. (H.C.Casserley)

55.   The signal box had 45 levers, opened with the line and closed on 13th August 1990. It was photographed in February 1985, when one of the old brown enamel signs was still to be seen. The footbridge was for the exclusive use of LT staff and was accidentally destroyed by a crane on 28th January 1995. The track on the right was removed in May 1990 and the platform widened greatly. (P.G.Barnes)

56.   Running past the LT Depot is the 15.39 from Marylebone to Aylesbury on 8th October 1988. The car sheds were largely complete at the start of WWII and they were thus requisitioned by the Admiralty for war work. (S.P.Derek)

WEST OF WEST RUISLIP

57.   We now have two views from the road bridge outside the station entrance. The sidings here were added in 1942 to facilitate wartime traffic. We witness shunting on 29th September 1962 - the sidings were still in place forty years later, retained by the engineers. (T.Wright)

58.   No. 4472 *Flying Scotsman* slows to enter the station on 4th May 1986, while working "The Shakespeare Limited" from Stratford-upon-Avon to Marylebone. The brake van is standing on the connection between BR and LT, over which new Underground rolling stock is delivered. (S.P.Derek)

59.   The water troughs were 560yds in length and were of great value in minimising journey times between London and Birmingham. No. 4068 *Llanthony Abbey* is working the 3.30pm Wolverhampton to Paddington on 22nd August 1931. With the water 8ins deep, about 2000 gallons could be scooped up at 40-50mph. (K.Nunn/LCGB)

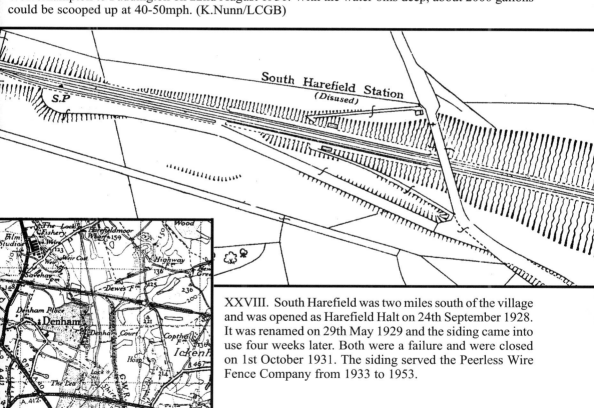

XXVIII. South Harefield was two miles south of the village and was opened as Harefield Halt on 24th September 1928. It was renamed on 29th May 1929 and the siding came into use four weeks later. Both were a failure and were closed on 1st October 1931. The siding served the Peerless Wire Fence Company from 1933 to 1953.

XXIX. The 1945 edition at 1ins to 1 mile has the closed station top right. There had been a curve to the left of it until 1917, to form a triangular junction with the Uxbridge branch, but it carried no regular traffic.

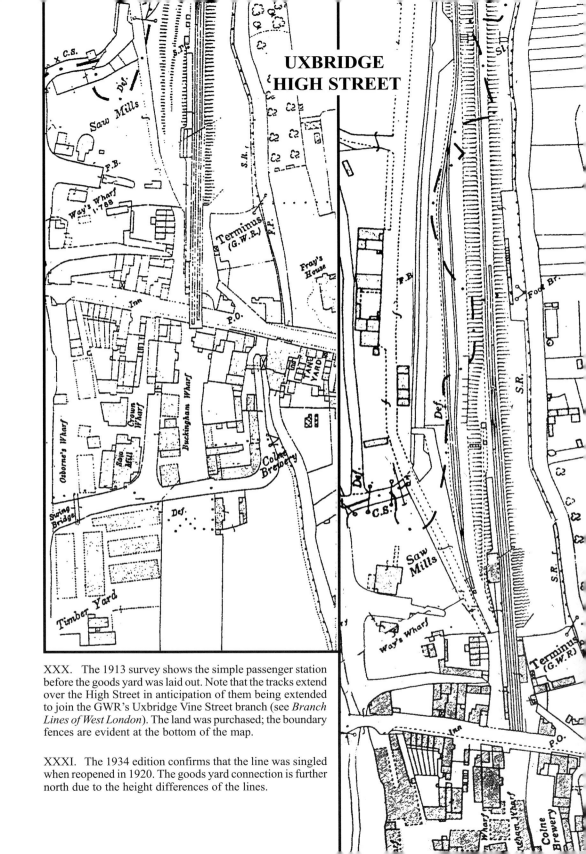

UXBRIDGE HIGH STREET

XXX. The 1913 survey shows the simple passenger station before the goods yard was laid out. Note that the tracks extend over the High Street in anticipation of them being extended to join the GWR's Uxbridge Vine Street branch (see *Branch Lines of West London*). The land was purchased; the boundary fences are evident at the bottom of the map.

XXXI. The 1934 edition confirms that the line was singled when reopened in 1920. The goods yard connection is further north due to the height differences of the lines.

60.   The GWR employed their new stanchion-free canopy design, which used long roof trusses. Seen when new, the entrance is on the left. The station was closed from January 1917 to May 1920. (Lens of Sutton)

61.   Two photographs from September 1948 both have glimpses of the goods yard on the left. This one includes the covered stairway to street level. Passenger trains had ceased on 1st September 1939. (P.J.Garland/R.S.Carpenter)

62.　　There was another trailing crossover behind the camera, although it is not shown on the map. The track on the right lasted until October 1956. (P.J.Garland/R.S.Carpenter)

63.　　Ex-GWR diesel railcar no. W13 stopped near the derelict structure on 26th September 1954, while on a railtour of Western branch lines. This was one of the first batch of 16 railcars produced. The streamlined bodies were built at Park Royal. (S.C.Nash)

64.　　The shunter stoops under the buffers while others pose for the photographer on 19th April 1958. No. 3750 is working the 8.25am freight to Denham, having had one numberplate stolen. However "81C" was still in place, this indicating Southall as its shed. (H.Davies)

65.　　Smoke rises from the brake van on 16th January 1964, as no. 5564 shunts the small yard. This was reported to be the last train, although the Esso depot siding was officially open until 1st January 1966. This was on the truncated eastern arm of the triangle. (T.Wright)

DENHAM

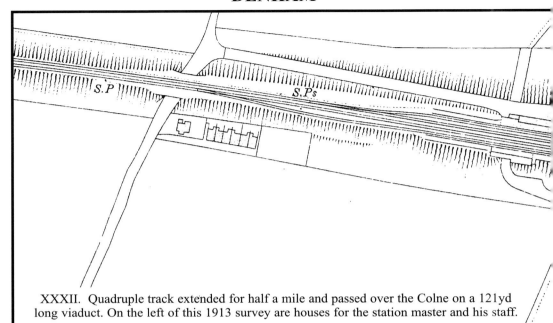

XXXII. Quadruple track extended for half a mile and passed over the Colne on a 121yd long viaduct. On the left of this 1913 survey are houses for the station master and his staff.

66. A standard design was used for most of the new stations and timber platforms were built on embankments to minimise weight on their shoulders. By 1929 there were 16 employees here. (Lens of Sutton)

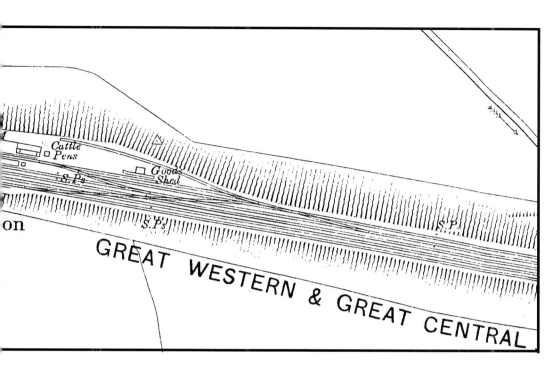

67.   In addition to the duty letter "C", steam railmotor no. 62 carries a destination board for "Paddington". It was built in 1906 and was one of a batch of 99 such vehicles completed in 1903-08. (R.S.Carpenter coll.)

68.   The through lines were removed in December 1965, the goods yard having closed on 6th January 1964. The 41-lever signal box was in use until 15th June 1975. The Uxbridge branch was controlled by Denham West Junction Box. This had 33 levers and closed on 13th December 1965. (Lens of Sutton coll.)

69.   The up side was recorded on 15th August 1985, little having changed to the structure. Some extra business had been generated by the presence of film studios nearby from 1939 to 1951: see map XXIX. (F.Hornby)

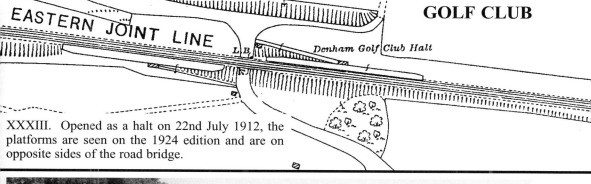

EASTERN JOINT LINE

L B

Denham Golf Club Halt

XXXIII. Opened as a halt on 22nd July 1912, the platforms are seen on the 1924 edition and are on opposite sides of the road bridge.

70.   The up platform (left) was rebuilt opposite the down one in June 1954. The two Pagoda shelters, seen in the 1960s, were still in service in 2002. (Lens of Sutton coll.)

71.   An up train bound for Marylebone runs in on 5th May 1961 behind 2-6-4T no. 42251, one of a batch of 4Ps started by the LMSR in 1945. Two men were employed here in the 1930s. (D.Trevor Rowe)

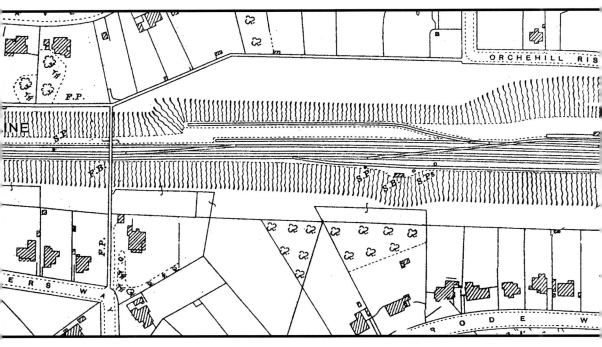

XXXIV. The 1924 survey shows the trackwork at its optimum and includes both signal boxes.

72.   An early postcard includes East Box, which closed on 11th November 1923. The white wooden staircase did not last long either. (Lens of Sutton)

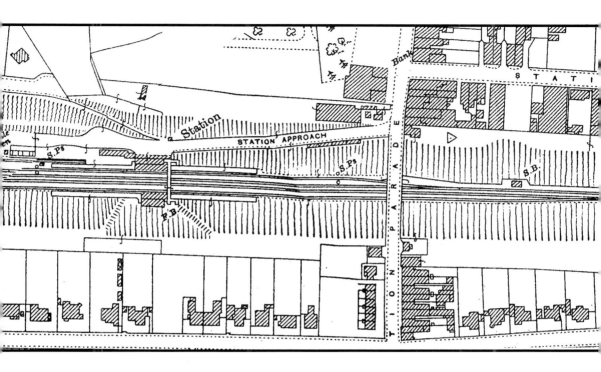

73. No. 6014 *King Henry VII* speeds through with the lengthy 6.30am Birkenhead to Paddington on 14th June 1958. There would soon be expresses every hour, when the Euston route was restricted due to electrification. (H.C.Casserley)

74.   Seen earlier in picture 71, no. 42251 is working to Marylebone on 7th May 1960. The grimy locomotive contrasts with the splendid Austin Sheerline. The crane was rated at 1½ tons, but little used by that time. The one in the next picture could lift five tons. (D.Trevor Rowe)

75.   No. 42159 pulls its down local service out of the loop on the same day. Goods traffic is in decline, the yard closing on 6th January 1964. In its final months, it handled coal only. (D.Trevor Rowe)

76.   No. 42230 arrives with an up local train on 5th May 1961 and passes the inelegant additional building which does not exist today. Note that cars have crept into the goods yard. (D.Trevor Rowe)

77.   The scene in June 1985 shows cars and puddles almost filling the former goods yard. The down DMU is passing the 33-lever signal box, which lasted until 10th August 1990. (T.Wright)

78.   No. 35028 *Clan Line* was attached at West Ruislip to a centenary special from Southend Victoria to Stratford-upon-Avon on 7th October 1989. The up platform was widened greatly and the remaining up line moved close to the down one. At the same time, a crossover and up refuge siding were added west of the station to allow trains from London to terminate. Four did so, Mondays to Fridays, in 2002. (S.P.Derek)

SEER GREEN

79.   Opened as "Beaconsfield Golf Links" on 1st January, it became simply "Seer Green" on 16th December 1918. The suffix "& Jordans" shown on the running-in board was in use between 1950 and 1974. (Lens of Sutton)

80.   An up DMU is about to stop on 7th July 1985, by which time "Jordans" was in favour again. The matching pair of buildings was still in use in 2002. The train will soon pass the site of Wilton Park signal box, which was in place in 1914-53. (T.Wright)

81.   Popularly known as the "Bin Liner", this train originated at the Hillingdon Waste Terminal mentioned in caption 49. It is being hauled by a class 45/0 on 3rd January 1987. Car parks now flank this station. (P.G.Barnes)

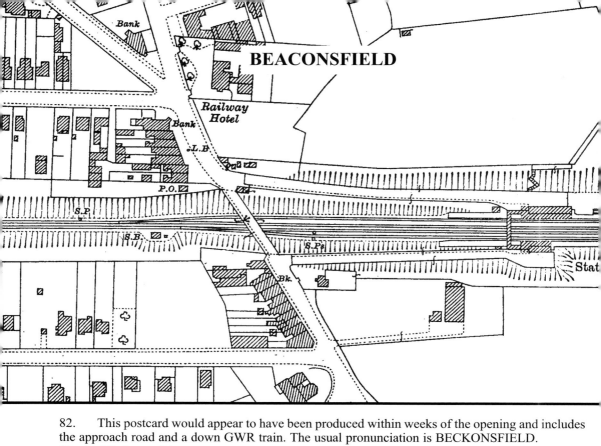

BEACONSFIELD

82.   This postcard would appear to have been produced within weeks of the opening and includes the approach road and a down GWR train. The usual pronunciation is BECKONSFIELD. (Lens of Sutton coll.)

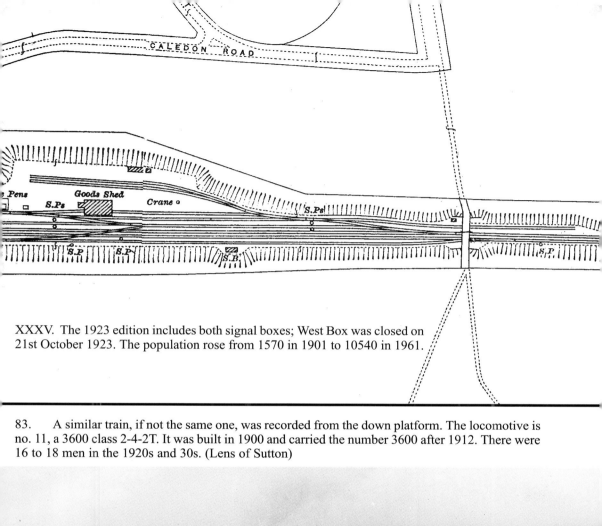

CALEDON ROAD

Pens

S.Ps

Goods Shed

Crane

S.Ps

S.P

S.P

S.B

S.P

XXXV. The 1923 edition includes both signal boxes; West Box was closed on 21st October 1923. The population rose from 1570 in 1901 to 10540 in 1961.

83.   A similar train, if not the same one, was recorded from the down platform. The locomotive is no. 11, a 3600 class 2-4-2T. It was built in 1900 and carried the number 3600 after 1912. There were 16 to 18 men in the 1920s and 30s. (Lens of Sutton)

84.   This shot of a 9000 class 4-4-0 in 1952 includes the cattle dock. A platform each side of the dock road was a feature of several stations on the route. See picture 67 for another example. (K.E.Fountain/GCRS)

85.   A 4300 class 2-6-0 was also photographed in 1952 and is about to pass under the bridge shown on the right of the map. It initially linked tracks across fields and has recently been replaced by a short concrete span, carrying only a footpath. (K.E.Fountain/GCRS)

86.   We can now enjoy a selection of typical trains on this part of the route in the 1950s. No. 4904 *Binnegar Hall* passes through on 2nd April 1955, with what is probably the 2.15pm Acton to Tyseley service. (B.W.Leslie/GCRS)

87.   No. 6165 is a 2-6-2T of the 6100 class and is hauling the 9.30am Princes Risborough to Southend-on-Sea excursion on 17th August 1958. Ten coaches containing buckets and spades are now difficult to imagine. (B.W.Leslie/GCRS)

88.   A more usual type of train is this up local to Marylebone in 1958. The coach next to the class L1 2-6-4T is ex-Great Central Railway. Fine pseudo-Tudor dwellings abound. (B.W.Leslie/GCRS)

89.   Speeding past the goods yard, which closed on 10th August 1964, is class K3 2-6-0 no. 61833. It is working the Marylebone-Perth car sleeper on 22nd June 1959. Most yards were provided with weighbridges of the type seen here. (B.W.Leslie/GCRS)

90.   BR class 4MT no. 76038 runs into the loop with Marylebone-Banbury milk empties on 6th July 1959. The centre roads were taken out of use on 30th December 1973 and the 39-lever signal box followed on 7th December 1975. Otherwise little has changed here. (B.W.Leslie/GCRS)

NORTH OF BEACONSFIELD

91.   Whitehouse Tunnel is 352 yards in length. Its northern portal is seen on 13th April 1959 as down empties emerge behind ex-WD 2-8-0 no. 90448. It will soon reach the site of Tylers Green signal box, which stood from 1914 to 1953 and had only six levers. (B.W.Leslie/GCRS)

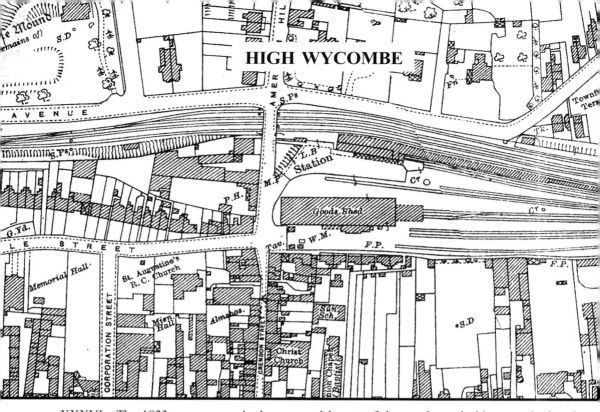

HIGH WYCOMBE

XXXVI. The 1923 survey reveals the cramped layout of the goods yard, this necessitating the provision of a supplementary one further west. The goods shed is on the site of the Wycombe Railway's first station and the flint walled parts probably date from 1854. It ceased to be a terminus in 1862, when a through station, with overall roof, was built at a slightly higher level in the position of the present down side buildings. The single line to Maidenhead is the lower one on the right. The station was simply "Wycombe" until 1864.

92.   The down side structures were built in 1906 and were still in use almost a century later. Downdraught on the hillside location must have beeen a problem, judging by the assortment of zinc cowls. (Lens of Sutton)

An earlier map and other photographs can be found in *Branch Lines to Henley, Windsor and Marlow.*

93.   To provide four tracks, it was necessary to cut back the sloping land and build the up platform further east. It is in the distance in this 1932 view, as is the water tank. This was erected on the site of a locomotive turntable that had been put there in 1892. The latter had previously been in the goods yard.
(Brunel University/Mowat coll.)

94.   BR class 4 2-6-4 T no. 80142 runs into the up platform on 4th August 1957, destined for Marylebone at 1.3pm. The staffing level had been 71 to 75 in the 1930s, reflecting the importance of this traffic centre. (B.W.Leslie/GCRS)

95.   A DMU from Marylebone arrives on 8th June 1978 and the points are set for the bay platform. Behind it is the remnant of the Maidenhead branch, closed in 1970 and still in place 30 years later as an engineers siding. The line on the left was added in 1943 to form a longer up loop. Marylebone controlled the area from 13th August 1990, but the 93-lever signal box continued to work the route north of the station until 6th March 1991. (T.Heavyside)

96.   Stopping trains terminate in the bay platform, this example being recorded on 16th February 1985. The photograph includes the run-round loop, disused since 1975 and lifted in 1989. (P.G.Barnes)

97.   The centre tracks had been removed during alterations of 1989-90. Two class 165 Turbos are seen on 28th July 1992; the one on the right is standing on reversible track and is near monitors provided for one person train operation. The other is in the bay once used by Maidenhead trains. (F.Hornby)

WEST OF HIGH WYCOMBE

98.   A view from Amersham Hill bridge, at the west end of the platforms, features the retaining wall (which required 1.25m bricks), and Middle Box, which lasted until 9th November 1972. Bulmer's Pullman cars are being hauled by no. 6000 *King George V* from Birmingham to Kensington (Olympia) on 4th October 1971 - the "Return to Steam" special. (M.J.Furnell)

99.   "The Shakespeare Limited" was also recorded at the end of the quadruple track, but on 18th May 1986. The eleven coaches were hauled from Marylebone to Stratford-upon-Avon by ex-SR no. 777 *Sir Lamiel*. (S.P.Derek)

100.   No. 47628 has the up through road signalled on 7th December 1988, as it rounds the curve towards the station with ballast wagons. The lamp man is seldom recorded in action. (M.J.Stretton)

XXXVII. West Box is included in this 1923 map; it closed on 7th October 1976. The upper track is a siding.

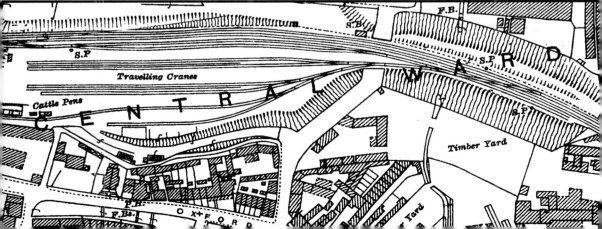

101.   A westward panorama from April 1957 includes West Box, Hughendon Road Viaduct (77yds), the 10-ton travelling crane and much of West Yard. It was in use from 1904 until 1966. The original single line viaduct was still in place, but out of view. (B.W.Leslie/GCRS)

102.   Ex-GWR 2-8-0 no. 3804 approaches West Box on 13th January 1962 with an up coal train. The strong demand for winter domestic fuel in the London conurbation brought a stream of such trains down the route; some, as this, via Banbury for west and south London yards. The Esso tank wagons (right) are standing on the industrial track which connected to the fuel depot a short way up the Hughenden Valley. There were two other sidings behind and parallel to the train from 1939 to 1976; they were known as "Chalk Sidings". (B.Jennings)

WEST WYCOMBE

103.   Space was provided, but the centre through lines were never laid. This southward view includes the signal box, which was in use until 24th April 1966. However, passenger services were withdrawn on 3rd November 1958 and freight followed on 4th February 1963. (Brunel University/Mowat coll.)

XXXVIII.   The 1919 edition. The crane (Cr.) was rated at six tons capacity. Although traffic generally diminished, staff rose thus: 3 in 1903, 9 in 1913, 12 in 1923 and 15 in 1936.

104.   One mile north of the station, there is a skew bridge over the A4010. Seen in 1970, it retained the abutments on the alignment of the original single line. (B.W.Leslie)

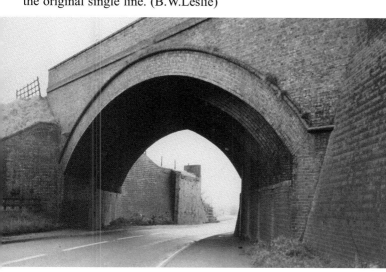

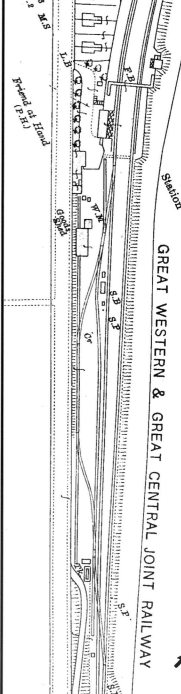

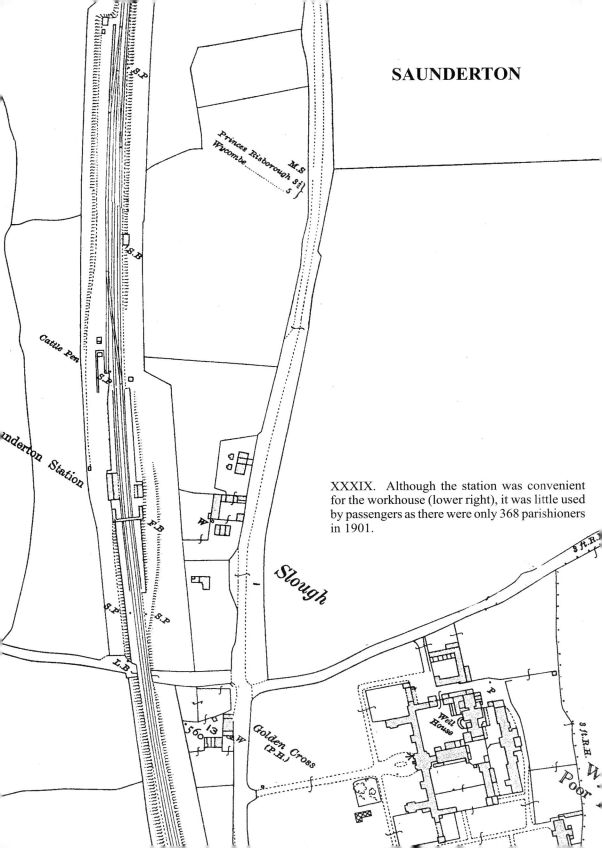

SAUNDERTON

Princes Risborough 3¾

Wycombe

M.S

5

S.P

S.B

Cattle Pen

S.P

.nderton Station

F.B

W

XXXIX. Although the station was convenient for the workhouse (lower right), it was little used by passengers as there were only 368 parishioners in 1901.

Slough

S.P

S.P

L.B

3 f. R.H.

.560

13

W

Golden Cross (P.H.)

Well House

P

3 f. R.H.

W

Pool

105.   A northward view in 1932 includes the signal box and goods yard, which closed on 1st March 1965. Five men were employed here in 1932. (Brunel University/Mowat coll.)

106.   Class V2 2-6-2 no. 60911 was of LNER origin and is working hard up the gradient on 27th December 1958, with the 12.15pm Marylebone to Manchester express. (B.W.Leslie/GCRS)

107.   We now have three photos taken on 20th December 1970. This was the main entrance, but the peeling notice offers a service against woodworm and dry rot. (B.W.Leslie/GCRS)

108.   A fire had destroyed the main building in 1913, but it appears that both were rebuilt soon afterwards. Nameboards seem absent in this southward view, but there are two seats present. (B.W.Leslie/GCRS)

109.   The box remained in use until 16th November 1975, having been built in about 1901. There had been a passing loop in single line days. (B.W.Leslie/GCRS)

110.   Grinding up the 1 in 164 incline on 13th July 1985 is the 17.40 (Saturdays only) Paddington to Stratford-upon-Avon. On other weekdays, the train ran to Birmingham and on those days only six down trains called here, but in peak hours only. None stopped at weekends. Chiltern Railways provided a minimum hourly service daily, a great improvement. (M.J.Stretton)

111.   A "Western" diesel hydraulic locomotive heads the 10.35am from Wolverhampton (LL) plus the 7.40am through coaches from Birkenhead (Woodside) through the steep chalk cutting south of Princes Risborough on 8th June 1963. The original route was too steep for a main line and opportunity was taken to ease this to 1 in 167 by adopting a separate southbound alignment, but this necessitated an 88yd long tunnel. (B.Jennings)

112.   The original single line is at a higher level than the 1905 up track. No. 34092 *City of Wells* is working hard on Saunderton Bank on 18th June 1988, with the "South Yorkshireman". This was a return trip from Marylebone to Sheffield, calling at Denham, Banbury and Derby. It had run to Stratford-upon-Avon seven days earlier. (D.Trevor Rowe)

113.   The two tracks converge south of the station and the 11.15 Marylebone to Banbury is about to cross to the platform road on 11th November 1989. The boundary fences come to a point above the rear coach. (P.G.Barnes)

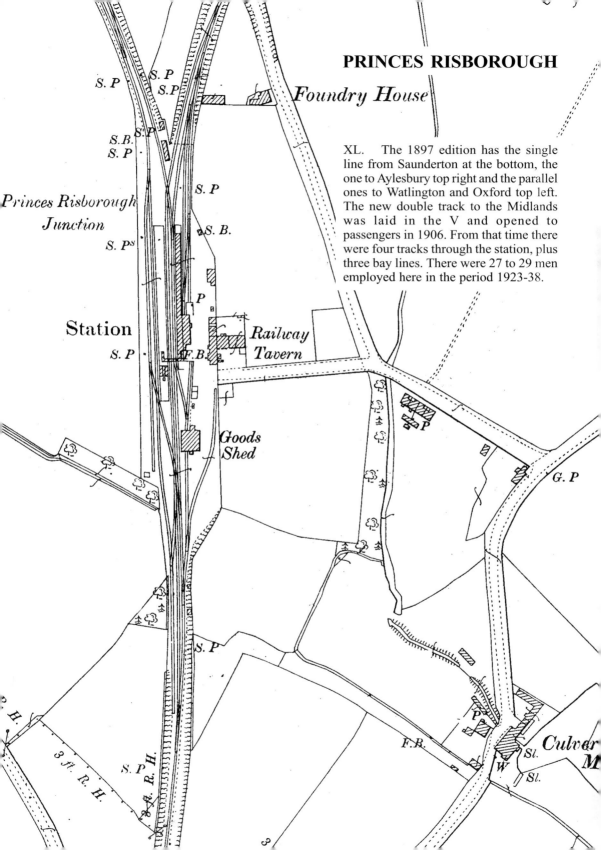

PRINCES RISBOROUGH

Foundry House

XL. The 1897 edition has the single line from Saunderton at the bottom, the one to Aylesbury top right and the parallel ones to Watlington and Oxford top left. The new double track to the Midlands was laid in the V and opened to passengers in 1906. From that time there were four tracks through the station, plus three bay lines. There were 27 to 29 men employed here in the period 1923-38.

Princes Risborough Junction

Station

Railway Tavern

Goods Shed

G. P

Culver M

114.   Bearing LNER on its tender, class B1 4-6-0 no. 1109 plods south with coal on 26th July 1947. Watlington trains to and from the bay passed behind the signal box. (H.C.Casserley)

115.   The footbridge was paradise for the steam observer. A down train passes North Box on 19th July 1952, as no. 6016 *King Edward V* races south with the 8.55am Birkenhead to Paddington and a crowd on the up platform waits for a stopping train. (H.C.Casserley)

Handbill from August 1955.

WALKING TOURS

DAY RETURN TICKETS

WILL BE ISSUED FROM

PADDINGTON

ON

Week-days and Sundays

(UNLESS OTHERWISE SHEWN)

UNTIL FURTHER NOTICE

AVAILABLE BY ANY TRAIN, SAME DAY, IN EACH DIRECTION

TO	Day Return Fares (Third Class).	TO	Day Return Fares (Third Class).
	s. d.		s. d.
*BEACONSFIELD (for Penn)	5/10	POYLE (for Stanwell Moor) HALT ...	4/10
BOURNE END	7/2	*PRINCES RISBOROUGH (via Beacons-	
BURNHAM (Bucks)	5/8	field or Maidenhead)	9/2
COLNBROOK	4/8	‡*SAUNDERTON (via Beaconsfield or	
COOKHAM	7/2	Maidenhead)	8/4
‡COWLEY	4/2	*SEER GREEN	5/8
*DENHAM (for Harefield)	4/2	SLOUGH	5/2
*DENHAM GOLF CLUB PLATFORM	4/4	STAINES WEST	5/4
FURZE PLATT HALT	6/10	TAPLOW	6/2
*GERRARDS CROSS	4/10	‡UXBRIDGE (Vine Street)	4/4
*HIGH WYCOMBE (via Beaconsfield		*WEST DRAYTON AND YIEWSLEY	3/10
or Maidenhead)	7/2	‡*WEST WYCOMBE (via Beaconsfield	
IVER	4/2	or Maidenhead)	7/8
LANGLEY (Bucks)	4/8	WINDSOR & ETON CENTRAL ...	5/10
LOUDWATER	7/2	WOOBURN GREEN	7/2
MAIDENHEAD	6/8	YEOVENEY	5/2
MARLOW	7/10		

*—The return halves of tickets issued to these Stations will be available to Paddington or to Marylebone via South Ruislip.

‡—Week-days only.

1st Class Fare 50% over Third Class Fare.

SPECIAL WALKING TOUR TICKETS.

Special Walking Tour Tickets will be issued daily (unless otherwise shewn), available by any train in each direction, as follows :—

No. of Tour	OUTWARD BY RAIL TO	RETURNING SAME DAY BY RAIL FROM	Walking Distance	Return Fares, Third Class.
			Miles.	s. d.
1	BEACONSFIELD	TWYFORD	16½	7/6
2	BOURNE END	TWYFORD	11	7/6
3	HENLEY-ON-THAMES	MARLOW	8½	8/6
4	SHIPLAKE	MARLOW	10	8/0
5	WARGRAVE	MARLOW	11	8/0
6	TWYFORD	MARLOW	12½	8/0
7	HIGH WYCOMBE	TWYFORD	13½	7/6
8	HIGH WYCOMBE	WARGRAVE	14	8/0
9	HIGH WYCOMBE	SHIPLAKE	16	8/0
10	HIGH WYCOMBE	HENLEY-ON-THAMES	12½	8/6
10a	HIGH WYCOMBE	AMERSHAM	7	7/3
10b	HIGH WYCOMBE	CHESHAM	8½	7/3
11	‡WEST WYCOMBE	TWYFORD	15	7/9
12	‡WEST WYCOMBE	WARGRAVE	15	8/0
13	‡WEST WYCOMBE	SHIPLAKE	14	8/0
14	‡WEST WYCOMBE	HENLEY-ON-THAMES	12	8/6
14a	WEST WYCOMBE	GREAT MISSENDEN	9	7/9
15	‡SAUNDERTON	TWYFORD	18	8/6
16	‡SAUNDERTON	WARGRAVE	17	8/6
17	‡SAUNDERTON	SHIPLAKE	17	8/6
18	‡SAUNDERTON	HENLEY-ON-THAMES	13½	8/6
19	PRINCES RISBOROUGH ...	HENLEY-ON-THAMES	20	9/3

‡—Available Week-days only.
NOTE.—Tickets for these tours may be taken in the reverse direction upon special application at the time of booking.

Children under Three years of age, Free ; Three and under Fourteen years of age, Half-fare.

116. North Box is seen above the leading van as 0-6-0PT no. 3608 works an up goods off the Oxford line on 23rd July 1955. On the left is the Forest Products Research Laboratory, which had private sidings from 1927 to 1971. (H.C.Casserley)

117. The Blue Pullman had diesel-electric power cars and was introduced on the Paddington to Wolverhampton route in September 1960. It ran non-stop (theoretically) south of Leamington Spa and was recorded on 19th March 1962. The coal on the left was for the Chinnor Cement Works, a traffic that ceased in December 1989. (B.Jennings)

118.   An April 1962 panorama includes the connection that went across all four running lines and linked to the "back road" (right) which allowed goods movements to be made clear of the passenger lines. The yard had a six-ton crane and closed on 10th October 1966. South Box (left of centre) closed on 23rd September 1966 and North Box had a panel added in 1968. (P.J.Garland/R.S.Carpenter)

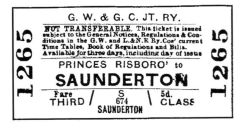

```
        G. W. & G. C. JT. RY.
1265   NOT TRANSFERABLE. This ticket is issued      1265
       subject to the General Notices, Regulations & Con-
       ditions in the G.W. and L.&N.E.Ry.Cos' current
       Time Tables, Book of Regulations and Bills.
       Available for three days, including day of issue.
        PRINCES RISBORO' to
        SAUNDERTON
         Fare  /    S     \   5d.
        THIRD  /   674    \  CLASS
             SAUNDERTON
```

```
         G. W. & G. C. Jt. Rly
512          FURLOUGH                            512
       FOR CONDITIONS SEE BACK.  Available for
          three days, including day of issue.
        RUISLIP GARDENS to
        EALING BROADWAY
            Via  Greenford
                 /  Fur. Sin. \
        THIRD    /     678     \    CLASS
            Ealing  Broadway
```

119.   The layout was drastically simplified in the Summer of 1968 and the down platform was eliminated. No. 56062 runs south on 11th November 1989 with aggregate for the Redland depot at Cricklewood. Three sidings were retained on the left for the engineers. (P.G.Barnes)

120.   The former 96-lever North Box closed on 6th March 1991, but was still standing ten years later, having been listed Grade II. No. 35028 *Clan Line* is seen with the 09.45 Marylebone to Stratford-upon-Avon on 22nd December 1990. As Chiltern Railways had enhanced the service to Birmingham, they provided a new down platform and footbridge in 1999. Services were improving and enterprise was evident, after years of decline. (S.P.Derek)

MP Middleton Press

Easebourne Lane, Midhurst, West Sussex.
GU29 9AZ   Tel:01730 813169
www.middletonpress.co.uk   email:info@middletonpress.co.uk

EVOLVING THE ULTIMATE RAIL ENCYCLOPEDIA

A-0 906520   B-1 873793   C-1 901706   D-1 904474

OOP Out of Print at time of printing - Please check current availability   **BROCHURE AVAILABLE SHOWING NEW TITLES**